Wannabe Backpackers

The Latin American & Kenyan Journey of Five Spoiled Teenagers

Gerald Yeung

Wannabe Backpackers tells the story of five self-confessed "spoiled teenagers" who travel to Latin America and Kenya one summer.

United by Gerald Yeung, the spiritual leader, the boys discover their true identity throughout the month-long journey: Justin the narcissist, Lulu the shopaholic, DJ the womanizer (or so he thought), and Brian the modern Romeo. From Machu Picchu in Peru to the Great Rift Valley of Kenya, they do every fun thing they can think of, with the sky the limit. "Reckless" becomes their common middle name.

At times, their patience and friendship are put to the test. Will they still be friends after ditching each other in a foreign country? Most important, will they eventually become backpackers?

Wannabe Backpackers

The Latin American & Kenyan Journey of Five Spoiled Teenagers

Gerald Yeung

Proverse Hong Kong

Gerald Yeung, Wannabe Backpackers

Wannabe Backpackers: The Latin American & Kenyan Journey of Five Spoiled Teenagers
by Gerald Yeung, 11 March 2009
First published in Hong Kong by Proverse Hong Kong in March 2009.
Web site: www.geocities.com/proversehk
© Proverse Hong Kong, 11 March 2009
ISBN 978-988-17724-2-8

Distribution: Hong Kong and worldwide from Hong Kong: The Chinese University Press of Hong Kong, The Chinese University of Hong Kong, Shatin, New Territories, Hong Kong, SAR. Email: <cup@cuhk.edu.hk>. Website: <www.chineseupress.com>.
Tel: [INT+852] 2609-6508; Fax: [INT+852] 2603-7355.
Distribution: United Kingdom and worldwide except Hong Kong from the UK: Enquiries and orders to Christine Penney, 28 West Street, Stratford-upon-Avon, Warwickshire CV37 6DN, UK. Email: <clodpoll2001@yahoo.com>
Additional distribution: Proverse Hong Kong, P.O. Box 259, Tung Chung Post Office, Tung Chung, Lantau Island, New Territories, Hong Kong, SAR.
E-mail: <proverse@netvigator.com>. Web site: <www.geocities.com/proversehk>

Moral Rights: The right of Gerald Yeung to be identified as the author of this book has been asserted by him in accordance with the Copyright, Designs and Patents Act 1988.

Printed in Hong Kong.
Page design, copy-editing & proof-reading by Proverse Hong Kong.
Cover design by David Szabo.
Back cover photograph by Justin Wong.
Photograph permissions may be requested from Proverse Hong Kong.

All rights reserved. No part of this publication may be reproduced, stored in a retrieval system, or transmitted in any form or by any means, electronic, mechanical, photocopying, recording or otherwise, without the prior written permission of the copyright owner.
The book is sold subject to the condition that it shall not, by way of trade or otherwise, be lent, re-sold, hired out or otherwise circulated without the publisher's prior written consent in any form of binding or cover other than that in which it is published and without a similar condition including this condition being imposed on the subsequent owner or purchaser. Please request, in writing, any and all permissions from Proverse Hong Kong.

Proverse Hong Kong
      British Library Cataloguing in Publication Data
  Yeung, Gerald Christopher, 1986-
  Wannabe Backpackers: the Latin American & Kenyan journey
  of five spoiled teenagers.
  1. Young adults--Travel--Latin America. 2. Young
  adults--Travel--Kenya. 3. Latin America--Description and
  travel. 4. Kenya--Description and travel.
  I. Title
  916.7'62'0443-dc22

  ISBN-13: 9789881772428

Author's Acknowledgments

I'd like to thank my publisher Proverse, Dr Gillian Bickley, and everyone involved in the making of this book, for the time and the heart they have devoted, and for the risk they undertook to promote an unknown author. You have changed my life.

Warm thanks to Josephine and Alfred for their tremendous work on the photos, and to aspiring artist, Kimberly for taking in hand my original attempt at presenting our journey in a sketch map and making it look so good.

I am most grateful to David Szabo for his work on the cover-design.

Thank you to Justin, Pierre, Lulu and Brian, for reading through this journal at an early stage and giving the go-ahead for its publication. You all can take a good joke and I love you for that. Thank you for the photographs you took, some of which are included in this book.

Special thanks to Johara for the booking at the Marriott Hotel. We could not have survived otherwise. Amy, thank you for arranging the tickets for us. Without your help, none of this would have happened.

To everyone whom we met along the way—I may not be able to name you all (I never knew some of your names)—thank you for being part of our experience and making it special. I hope we did the same for you.

Many of the photographs were taken by strangers with one of our own cameras. We never knew your names. Thank you for your help in preserving our happy memories.

Most important, we owe our parents a big "thank you", for the sacrifices they made to broaden our horizons, giving us privileges that they never enjoyed.

Lastly, to Justin, Pierre, Lulu and Brian, thank you for sharing this wonderful experience that I will forever cherish.

Dedication

To our families—
for the sacrifices they made to broaden our horizons.
They gave us privileges they never themselves enjoyed.

"Thank you!"
(L to R) Brian, Lulu, Justin, Pierre, Gerald.
Forest of Iguazu, Argentina.

Gerald Yeung, Wannabe Backpackers

Gerald's Introduction

It was one casual Saturday afternoon at our favourite soccer field. It is normally hard to convince the likes of Lulu to play soccer on a cold early January afternoon, but in the spirit of brotherhood, we decided to get together once more before going back to our respective universities for another six months. Between the laughs and giggles, we talked about girls. Then we made fun of our friend, "Chicken". Finally, we started making plans for the coming summer. It was all boring talk about summer internships and we were about to go back to making fun of Chicken again, when someone made a harmless but ultimately historic suggestion, "Why don't we travel together this summer?"

We had had this idea for ages. Travelling is great. The only bad thing about it is that you have to see your parents and younger siblings twenty-four/seven. When we were younger, we often fantasized about being able to travel without having to visit museums with our parents, but our dreams were always cruelly swallowed by the reality that there was no chance our parents would let us venture into unknown and potentially dangerous foreign domains, somewhere off their radar. But when the suggestion was brought up once again that afternoon, the melody of those words and their associating thoughts resonated in our ears, and it suddenly dawned upon us that we were about to turn twenty, an age that will allow you to get married, fight in a war, watch movies full of adult concepts, go to jail, and basically make any life decision there is. In short, we were adults, and we were entitled to freedom. What had previously prevented us from materializing our dream was no longer an obstacle. Then I mentioned the glorious invention of Around the World Tickets, which allow you to make as many stops as you want around the world as long as you keep travelling in one direction. And we knew that we would be going around the world that summer. We would make it happen at all costs.

Gerald Yeung, Wannabe Backpackers

During the following five months, we came up with millions of ideas for destinations. Due to the vastness of the globe and indecisiveness on our part, we only managed to eliminate countries that were too dangerous because of wars or epidemics. The idea of going wherever we want sounded simple (pick your favorite countries!), but when you have to plan out a month-long trip for the first time in your life, you discover all sorts of scheduling conflicts and other complications previously unseen in the teenage world. I was actually glad that space travel had yet to be developed, otherwise my hair might have turned white overnight.

After much procrastination and complaining, we did make some progress. Lulu and I did look for a safari tour and hostels and I did decide on the destinations and dates based on my personal preferences only. And I did find a random travel agent online by the name Belize (that might not be the actual name, but at school I was learning about Belize, the country, at that time): and he had the entire trip planned out for us until my mother decided at the last minute that she wouldn't trust her credit card number with a person who shares a name with a Caribbean country. In the end, whether our trip would happen or not ultimately came down to one person—my mother's secretary, who should now be titled Amy the Great for booking our plane tickets (there were about fifteen individual flights for each person). Without her coming to the rescue, it could still be all talk today.

In terms of stealing ten thousand US dollars (our projected budget) from our parents to sponsor this trip, we used the fact that we were all turning twenty as leverage. That was a great amount of money in everyone's book, but each of us made our own bargain with our parents. I didn't know what the others did, but for me, I made a pact with my mother that in return, I would keep a journal. I don't usually follow the rules laid out by any contracts between my mother and myself, but somehow I did this time, which led to the eventual appearance of this book. I guess this might be one of those rare occasions where parents are actually right. Maybe also, subconsciously, I was a writer in the making.

Why did we visit the places we did?

When I asked my friends for ideas, they were infinitely prolific. Egypt, Dubai, Turkey, Mongolia, Sierra Leone, the North Pole, Cuba, Venus. . . . At some point I felt that they were just naming places off the top of their heads without giving any thought to the tourist aspect of our discussion. And when the time came for decision-making, they all turned off their phones and disappeared altogether from the face of the Earth. Weeks of collective effort by five college students produced only five rough guidelines. They were as follows:
- We wanted to begin and end our journey in our home, Hong Kong;
- We wanted to go on an African safari;
- We wanted to go to the Caribbean;
- We wanted to go to South America;
- We will go through wherever it takes to visit the above places.

The virtue of our rough guidelines, which also happened to be their shortcoming, was that they were very rough—they didn't specify any country at all. So in theory, we could choose among several thousand routes that fulfilled all five of the agreed criteria. Such is our usual incompetence when it comes to decision-making. So one Saturday night, I turned down all party invitations and stayed in my room; and, in an attempt to separate fantasy from reality, worked out a route.

Since our families all live in Hong Kong, the logical thing to do would be to start and end our journey there, so that we can eat our parents' delicious cooking before and after our trip. It would also provide the perfect platform for our younger siblings to welcome us home with a standing ovation at Hong Kong Airport. At which point we would drop our bags to receive flowers and gifts and allow them to express their admiration, because by then we would have survived a month of absolute independence.

Of all the places on Earth, South America was the least travelled among people we know. And yet we always thought that we had acquired a fairly thorough understanding of it through the sport of soccer, and this was why we all wanted to go there. In particular, we wanted to see Machu Picchu. No, *I* wanted to see Machu Picchu, and I made the others come with me. The first time I saw photographs of the ancient Inca city in a book, I was instantly mesmerized by its glamour and promised myself that before I die I must walk on that unearthly green grass. To get to Machu Picchu, we had to go through Lima and Cusco, which were also among the most popular destinations in South America, according to travel books. These decided on, we had the whole Peru part of the trip planned out for us.

Another South American country that has always tickled my curiosity was Argentina. Prior to the trip, our understanding of Argentina was limited to their soccer players, who all seemed to be born with nice long hair in addition to magical footwork. Coincidentally, we (actually, it was mostly Justin and me) were going through that stage in every male upbringing when we considered having long hair the next coolest thing after Cristiano Ronaldo. Therefore, a trip to Argentina couldn't go too wrong. Even if we failed to verify that all Argentine males have long hair, at least we would get to play some Argentinian soccer.

Another popular destination in Argentina, according to Lulu, is Iguazu Falls. He learned this from his father, who visited Iguazu Falls once and has since recommended it as, "one of the most beautiful natural sights in the world." Enlightened by the wisdom of a frequent traveller, we packed an extra rain-jacket to go to the Falls.

Gerald Yeung, Wannabe Backpackers

The planning of the Caribbean part of the trip was extremely annoying simply because there are so many islands in that area. This is why the way most people do it, or the way most *old* people do it, is to take a cruise around the Caribbean. We obviously didn't want to be stuck on a cruise with other people's grandparents, because it sounded boring and expensive. We would never have gone through all that trouble to go to the Caribbean if it hadn't been for its reputation for having the nicest beaches and oceans, which is what we young people are all about. But the true gems behind the white sand and blue ocean are, as any straight guy would agree, the Caribbean girls, who are blessed with an angelic beauty beyond imagination. Dreaming about these girls was satisfying, but it didn't help our planning in any way. We thought our Caribbean dream would fall through until one day Lulu mentioned Margarita Island. We thought he was just making something up to be funny.

"Oh, really? Let's go to Tequila Island too, unless you prefer Long Island Iced Island. Ha, I just said two 'islands' in a roll," said the sarcastic voices of the rest of us.

"No, I am serious, guys, I read in some books and magazines that local Venezuelans often take weekend trips to that island. So it is probably the most convenient and economical way to go to the Caribbean."

The reason he brought this up was because, to go from South America to Africa (remember guideline number two?), we had to go through Miami and London, and to go to Miami from South America we had to go through Caracas, Venezuela. So, with the knowledge that we could spend a few days in Venezuela, he did some research and discovered this island named after a girlie drink.

To be honest, I had my doubts at first. Over our fifteen years of friendship, Lulu had never established himself in my eyes as a reader. But as soon as he used the word "economical", we all seconded his notion. After all, we were all about the money.

Gerald Yeung, Wannabe Backpackers

We applied similar (economically-driven) logic to planning our African safari trip. Much to my dismay, there are probably as many African safaris as there are beach resorts in the Caribbean. (Actually, having said this, I am not sure if it is true, but there surely are more than one would think, off the top of one's head.) But if you eliminate all the unnecessarily extravagant safaris on offer (more than US$500 per person per night), you are left with a few choices of what they call "student safaris", which cost as little as US$500 a week. We signed up immediately.

With the price we were paying, we were not expecting luxury. The camping experience, however, still came much as a surprise, pleasant or not, you will soon find out. If we had known that we wouldn't see a bathroom for a week or that we would be fed a ration of food that makes third world countries look affluent, we would certainly have invested a few more bucks for a more civilized experience.

This was how we—I—came up with this route through seemingly random destinations. Some were destinations in themselves. Others were means to get to the places we really wanted to visit.

Table of Contents

Author's Acknowledgments	5
Dedication	6
Gerald's Introduction	7
Table of Contents	13
Table of Illustrations	14
The Characters	17
Itinerary	20
Prologue	21
The Journey Begins	21
The Red And Green Lights	25
A Decayed Colonial Heart	27
La Rosa Nautica	34
Sunniest Place on Earth	37
The Lost City	39
Corpus Cristi	44
Bar Crawl Two	48
Home Alone	51
Shampoo	55
Metrosexuals in the Making	60
Spoiled Kids versus Hostile Girl	64
A First Taste of Waterfall	67
Forces of Nature	70
Here Without You	76
Las Quinceañeras	80
Definition of Adventure	83
Butt Pirate of the Caribbean	87
Best Seafood in Miami	91
Don't Bother to Read	93
Business Class My Ass	94
A Day in London	96
We Didn't Sign Up For This	99
"Does Anyone Want to Pee?"	102

Totally Didn't Sign Up For This Either	106
Reefer	112
To Berlin!	115
The Proof of Manhood	119
In the World of Ostriches	124
A Casa	127
Pierre Speaks	128
Justin's Memories	131
Epilogue. Gerald resumes his Story	134
About the Author	141
The Portfolio	143
Glossary and Notes to Art, Games, History and Movies	152
Sources of information	155
Notes	155
Proverse Hong Kong Books	156
About Proverse Hong Kong	162
The Proverse Prize	163

Table of Illustrations

Thank you! Forest of Iguazu, Argentina....................	6
Outside Nairobi Airport, Kenya.............................	18
The Journey. Sketch-map.......................…...........	19
Guardian of Buenos Aires, Argentina......................	20
Here we go! Hong Kong Airport............................	24
Happy at Plaza Mayor, Lima, Peru.........................	33
Statue of Pachacutec. Cusco, Peru..........................	36
Ollyantas train station. Peru.	38
Feasting llamas. Machu Picchu, Peru.	42
Five guardian angels of Machu Picchu, Peru.	43
Before the sacred place. Machu Picchu, Peru..............	43
El Catedral. Cusco, Peru..	47
Machu Picchu the drink. Barranco, Lima, Peru............	50

Synchronized swimming. Marriott Plaza Hotel, Buenos Aires, Argentina... 54
Plaza de los Dos Congresos Parlament. Buenos Aires, Argentina... 54
Avenida Florida. Buenos Aires, Argentina................. 63
To the jungle. Iguazu, Argentina........................... 66
Tarzan is handsome, Tarzan is strong. Forest of Iguazu, Argentina... 69
The Iguazu Falls. Iguazu, Argentina....................... 74
The excursion. Iguazu, Argentina.......................... 75
No idea who she is! Iguazu, Argentina..................... 75
Gate Number Eleven. Buenos Aires, Argentina............ 79
In Wonderland. Margarita Island, Venezuela. 82
Ciao, Isla Margarita! Margarita Island, Venezuela......... 92
Millennium Wheel, London, UK............................ 95
The Houses of Parliament, London, UK.................... 95
Giraffe. Kenya... 98
Leopard lazing in a tree. Samburu, Kenya.................. 101
Mama and baby elephant. Samburu, Kenya................. 101
Even more like backpackers. Samburu, Kenya............. 104
Lake Nakuru. Nakuru, Kenya................................ 105
Great Rift Valley. Kenya..................................... 105
Zebra Socializing. Nakuru, Kenya.......................... 111
Buffalo. Lake Nakuru, Kenya................................ 111
Graceful lioness. Masai Mara, Kenya....................... 114
This is what happens when you lose in Bums. Masai Mara, Kenya... 117
Attentive cheetah. Masai Mara, Kenya..................... 118
The Great Migration. Masai Mara, Kenya 118
The man who slew a lion and a boy who believed it. Masai Mara, Kenya... 122
Club House of the Masai Mara campsite, Kenya........... 123
Two of my best friends: DJ and Soccer. Masai Mara, Kenya... 123

Gerald Yeung, Wannabe Backpackers

Back home in Hong Kong!................................	126
DJ Tree……………………………………………..	128
Justin. Lake Nakuru, Kenya………………………	130
We hope you will see us again! Margarita Island, Venezuela…………………………………………….	140

Portfolio

Columbian Señoritas. Margarita Island, Venezuela……..	143
She who sold me pyjamas. Aguas Calientes, Peru……….	144
Happy Times. Kamy Beach, Venezuela………………….	144
DJ. Cusco, Peru………………………………………..	145
Margarita Island, Venezuela……………………………..	145
DJ with a model. Kamy Beach, Venezuela………………	146
Pretty Peruvian girls. Ollyantas train station, Peru……….	146
Ms Mafe. Margarita Island, Venezuela…………………..	147
Ms Mafe. Kamy Beach, Venezuela………………………	148
Ms Esperenza. Margarita Island, Venezuela……………..	148
Margarita Island. We love Venezuela!................................	149
Justin. Lima, Peru………………………………………..	149
Cuba Libre of Iguazu, Argentina………………………...	150
Cuba Libre of Iguazu, Argentina………………………...	150
Gerald with Ms Scholars. Lima, Peru……………………	151
Even more like backpackers. Samburu, Kenya………….	Cover (front)
Final thoughts. Machu Picchu, Peru……………………..	Cover (back)

The Characters (*Please see photograph, "The Characters"*)

LOUIS "LULU" LAI (far left). Also known as "Mainland Man" who is obsessed with shopping. Possesses illegal travel documents. Student at The University of Wisconsin-Madison, majoring in Accounting.

PIERRE LAM (far right). Also known as DJ Tree. Finds satisfaction in deleting songs from iPods. Attracts girls of all ages. Student at The University of California at Berkeley, majoring in Economics.

BRIAN WONG (second to left). The baby of the group. Addicted to sugar. Consumes a daily Toblerone. Student at Carnegie Mellon University, majoring in Business.

JUSTIN WONG (centre). Obsessed with wrestling. A PSP addict. Never smiles in pictures. Student at The London School of Economics and Political Science, majoring in Accounting and Finance.

GERALD YEUNG (second to right). The sage, the grandmaster, the warrior and the author of this journal. Student at Cornell University, majoring in Mechanical and Aerospace Engineering.

The Characters

*(L to R) Lulu, Brian, Justin, Gerald, Pierre.
Outside Nairobi Airport, Kenya.*

The Journey

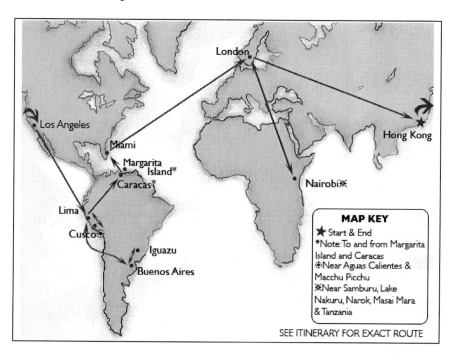

The Itinerary

JUNE
8th: Hong Kong to Los Angeles
9th: Los Angeles to Lima
10th: Lima
11th: Lima
12th: Lima to Cusco
13th: Cusco to Aguas Calientes to Machu Picchu
14th: Aguas Calientes to Cusco
15th: Cusco to Lima
16th: Lima to Buenos Aires
17th: Buenos Aires
18th: Buenos Aires
19th: Buenos Aires to Iguazu
20th: Iguazu
21st: Iguazu
22nd: Iguazu to Buenos Aires to Lima
23rd: Lima to Caracas to Margarita Island
24th: Margarita Island
25th: Margarita Island
26th: Margarita Island to Caracas to Miami
27th: Miami
28th: Miami to London
29th: London to Nairobi
30th: Nairobi to Samburu

JULY
1st: Samburu
2nd: Samburu to Lake Nakuru
3rd: Lake Nakuru to Narok, Masai Mara
4th: Masai Mara
5th: Masai Mara to Tanzania to Masai Mara
6th: Masai Mara to Nairobi
7th: Nairobi to London to Hong Kong

Guardian of Buenos Aires. Argentina. Photo by Brian.

Prologue

Five teenagers, twenty years of age, with fifty thousand US dollars, flew thirty-nine thousand seven hundred and thirty-five miles, eighty-five hours, on sixteen flights, set foot in five continents, eight countries, sixteen cities, took a thousand and fifty-six pictures, saw thirty World Cup games, tasted twelve types of beer, and stole the hearts of N girls in thirty days. The statistics combined to make a life-changing experience.

8th June
Cloudy
Hong Kong to Los Angeles

The Journey Begins
A good traveller has no fixed plans and is not intent on arriving.—Lao Tzu

It had been a long wait—the past six months felt like eternity—but when the day finally arrived, we could hardly imagine it happening. On this special day, the five of us, Justin, Brian, Pierre, Lulu, and I, embarked on an epic journey, spreading love to every corner of the planet. Due to our insufficient preparation, we had no idea what we were doing. It was quite a miracle that this trip happened in the end. There could not have been more last-minute arrangements, some of which probably would not work out. But that could be dealt with later. This was the day when our dream came true.

The story begins at Hong Kong International Airport. I am sure no-one has ever been checked in as slowly as we were. But it was partly our fault because we continually flirted with the check-in attendant.

"Wow, are you guys going all over South America?" she

asked in a tone of jealousy upon seeing five piles of tickets.

"Pretty much," I replied.

Just as I was about to ask for her number, I remembered something more important that we needed from her: a free upgrade to business class. Given our irresistible charisma and caramel sweet-talking, she willingly put two of us in business class. For the past few months, while swimming among images of the wonderful experiences about to be unveiled before our eyes, I was also anticipating conflict among us. It turned out that conflict arose surprisingly sooner than I had thought. Which two lucky boys would be excused from the next twelve hours of agony?

The conflict was settled by the simplest means: rock, paper, scissors. In the coming weeks together, this game would be used as the ultimate mediator in any conflict. For now, Brian and I were the winners. But I gave away my spot because I didn't really mind sitting with Lulu and Pierre in economy.

We needed a picture to commemorate our embarkation so we asked a passer-by to perform the honours. Not looking much of a photographer, he decided to shoot from a very low angle. This sent chills down Justin's spine as his biggest fear was to look fat in pictures. It wasn't that he was skinny to begin with.

Before boarding, we loaded our bags with tons of candies and fifty low-taste magazines. Unfortunately, like other teenagers in Hong Kong, we were superficial individuals.

Lulu, Pierre and I were stuck with each other for half a day. Instead of cursing our bad luck, we provided each other with ample entertainment and ended up being happy about the arrangement. We watched a movie, ate, and played cards for five hours straight. Just for your information, there would be 80+ hours of flying ahead of us and I doubt that we possessed the powerful creativity to make them any less painful. It was just another hurdle we needed to jump. Justin stopped by to say Hi with two hours left to tell us about the ten-hour coma he just woke up from. Meanwhile, Brian decided to abandon his friends and continued to indulge in the comforts of business-class privileges.

"Sure, we will switch with you guys halfway through," promised Brian before we boarded.

Los Angeles

Two hours after getting off the plane, I was sitting in the secondary customs of LA airport with our first stop of the trip already in jeopardy. Apparently Lulu hadn't brought the necessary documents to validate his student visa.

"Do you know what the guy at the customs told me?" asked Lulu.

"Tell me," I said. Even though I knew for sure that he was not about to tell me anything pleasant, I was willing to listen. Whatever Lulu says is always respectably amusing.

"I tried to make up stories to justify the disappearance of the documents, but he interrupted and said, 'You are in trouble.'"

When a tactful officer uses strong words like "trouble", it is never a good sign. So I decided to stay with Lulu while the rest of the party proceeded to Pierre's place. Although we always tease each other with extremely sarcastic remarks, in times of crisis (like the one we were currently living through) we are really helpful and composed. No-one points a finger. I had expected trouble, so I was not particularly worried. Sleeping at the terminal for a night shouldn't be bad. If Tom Hanks could do it, why couldn't I? To think on the bright side, it would be a good time to write my diary, to obtain random video footage, and to challenge the authority of the "world police," whom I bitterly despised. Justin had even joked with us before he left by asking Lulu to look after me and to make sure I wouldn't bite people.

We ended up staying at the airport for six hours until 8 or 9pm. Lulu told us that they threatened to send him back to Hong Kong and to blacklist him so that he would have to endure similar turmoil every time he set foot on American soil. I could picture the expressions on his parents' faces when they opened the door

Gerald Yeung, Wannabe Backpackers

tomorrow and found their beloved son saying, "Hi, Mum and Dad, I am back. Surprise!" Pretty certainly they would murder him. Although that didn't happen, we could read Lulu's worries on his face. Coming out of the office, he had aged but he refused to recount the details of the "interview." It could not be more obvious that he had bribed his way out with the unspeakable sacrifice, but no-one uttered a word.

In retrospect, it is ironic how Lulu had insisted that we should obtain the necessary visas prior to the trip but it was he who turned out to be the one who most needed admonition.

"You US passport people, be sure to get your documents. Otherwise I'll be having fun alone in Kenya while you guys live in the airport for a week," said Lulu exactly two weeks ago. Life comes at you pretty fast.

Finally, we had supper at a Chinese restaurant, played pool and went to Pierre's brother's studio to sleep. He was a kind host. We showered and went to sleep right away after a long day.

Here we go!
(L to R) Justin, Lulu, Brian, Pierre, Gerald.
Hong Kong Airport.

9th June
Cloudy
Los Angeles to Lima

The Red and Green Lights
Peculiar travel suggestions are dancing lessons from God.
    — Kurt Vonnegut Jnr.

Seeing the world came at a great cost—we missed the first day of the World Cup, a huge sacrifice for us soccer fans. Before going to the airport, we enriched the grocery store. Soap, shampoo, conditioner, lotion, hair bleach, vitamin C.... The long list would hopefully make up for our substandard preparation. While we were having overpriced Japanese food at the airport, we caught Pierre playing with a little girl in diapers in a most motherly manner. He would make a great father, but I am more content to be his friend.

The flight wasn't bad at all. LAN Chile offered a much more comfortable flight than Cathay. Justin and I were playing *Who wants to be a Millionaire* for a while before watching *Fun with Dick and Jane* and part of *The Lion, The Witch, and The Wardrobe*. Eight hours went by fast.

Customs and luggage claiming were surprisingly efficient, at least in comparison with most airports in the US. I guess you should be more careful about letting in people when the entire world hates you. We had to present our luggage tags to claim ownership of our bags. The final clearance required all passengers to push a button that randomly triggered one of the two lights (green and red). Green meant free to go; red required a luggage scan and further inspection. Everyone had green except for Brian. I decided to go right after him, figuring that the red wouldn't go off twice consecutively. But the story of my life is written as a comic tragedy. I had to go through a secondary scan too. I hoped it wasn't an early indication that my luck was bad.

Gerald Yeung, Wannabe Backpackers

As prearranged, a driver drove us to the hotel. Besides providing transportation, he also entertained our questions on Lima. Unfortunately for Pierre and Justin, my limited vocabulary was unable to translate their questions on prostitution and gambling. Our hotel, Hotel Esperanza, hardly provided what we would expect from a hotel. We stayed in a room with five beds and a tiny bathroom. Mini-safe, TV, fridge and hot water were all missing in action. Why was I not surprised? The lack of hot water implied that a lot of us would not be showering in the next few days. This should give you an idea of how spoiled we were. How were we going to last a month? That remained the question in everyone's mind but no-one was willing to voice their concern.

Our hotel was situated in Miraflores, a popular bar and restaurant district for tourists. Now that our parents were thousands of miles away, we could do whatever we wanted. It was past 2am, but who said we couldn't go out? We went to a pub right across from our hotel for a few beers. The major brands of beer in Peru are Cusqueña, Pilsen, Cristal and Cusqueña Malta. Cusqueña is the smoothest of all while Cusqueña Malta is essentially a thick, dark paste. Consumption of this beverage indicates malfunctioning taste-buds and a tendency towards self-destruction. I obtained info from the bartender on locations where it was possible to watch the World Cup, but Justin accused me of making an excuse to flirt with the man.

Gerald Yeung, Wannabe Backpackers

10th June
Cloudy
Lima

A Decayed Colonial Heart
If no man could become rich in Peru, no man could become poor.—William Prescott

We planned to wake up at 8am to watch both World Cup matches at the Brazilian restaurant the bartender recommended.

Unfortunately, unexpected circumstances caused us to deviate from the original plan. The electricity went out twice within half an hour and left people screaming in the shower because lights and water heaters don't run without electricity.

What characterizes us humans is that we make mistakes. They come in different forms, some more avoidable than others. One of the most avoidable is bad decision-making: doing the wrong thing at the wrong moment. For example, hair bleaching the first thing in the morning is an example of poor judgment and sheer stupidity. It would be an insult to amateurs to call it an amateur mistake. Figuratively, it is suicide from the point of view of fashion. What surprised me, though, was that it was Justin Wong the narcissist, of all people, who pulled his own plug. First, he underestimated the strength of the bleach. He also forgot to take into account that Lulu took half an hour to brush his teeth. When Justin walked out of the shower, I could hear thousands of curse words coming alarmingly from an infuriated boy, sporting flaming brown hair adorned with irregular patches of unintentional highlights. If Justin had come on this trip just for the chicks, the events of that morning could well be the end of his journey.

We finally left our room. But as soon as we stepped out of the building, we began another heated debate on why the hotel kept our room key. All these delays resulted in an arrival at the restaurant three hours later than intended. I was about to ask the waitress whether they were showing the England match when she told me the result (one to nil, England). Apparently, Mr. Bartender had told us the wrong time and so we had to settle with Sweden vs. Trinidad & Tobago, a less appealing fixture. We hardly understood anything on the Portuguese menu, so we ordered whatever the lady recommended. The food was far from good and the match was less than exciting. We eventually left the restaurant at half time with the game scoreless. What went on in the street was way more interesting. A group of bikers cruised around the periphery of the neighborhood. Some were in spandex, some in superhero costumes and some were bare-ass naked. It seemed like a Peruvian Tour de France, but the cops that chased down the bikers ruled out that possibility. It could be the underground version. The police made several arrest attempts, but the bikers simply disregarded them and carried on. Although these rebels may not be a good representation of the population, they portrayed our first impression of Peru: a country of free will.

It is time to talk about our expectations; what we planned to achieve. Besides broadening our horizons, we also hoped to challenge ourselves to do bold things. In particular, chatting up girls at random is always a handy technique to have under the belt. Therefore, we held a competition to see how many different girls we could persuade to be photographed with us. Any female between the age of fifteen and sixty was fair game. The age-limit affected no-one but Pierre because his love seemed to know no age boundary.

Lima, the capital of Peru, was founded in 1535 by the Spanish conquistador Francisco Pizarro. It was also known as La Ciudad de los Reyes (The City of Kings). Representing the heart of a colonial empire, Lima witnessed the rise and fall of Spanish rule, which eventually ended in the early 1800s. Nonetheless, traces of colonialism still linger on in Lima's architecture, culture and people.

Gerald Yeung, Wannabe Backpackers

    Our first stop was Plaza Mayor, also known as Plaza de Armas. Beside its European architecture, the Plaza will also be remembered as the place where I activated the scoreboard for our little competition. Two girls approached me and asked several questions in Spanish. They wanted to know more about children in poverty from a tourist's perspective (at least that was what I reckoned they were asking). I told them that I had only just arrived the night before and hadn't seen enough to make a fair comment but they didn't seem satisfied. So I tried my best to give them a typical description of children living in poverty. My cooperation came with a price, a picture. They merrily accepted.

    The Plaza Mayor is the most history-cultivated district in Lima. The Peruvian government palace and the Metropolitan Municipality of Lima (City Hall) are two of the Plaza's elegant structures. El Catedral lies on the eastern side of the square. I was overwhelmed by the austere architecture and intricate details of the cathedral's interior. The lofty ceiling inspired a feeling of the presence of a higher authority in that house of God. Had I been on my own, I would have allotted more time to giving accolades to the men who erected the church and allowing the sacred atmosphere to cleanse my mind. Surprisingly, Pierre shared the same desire for mind-cleansing, but I told him that he had been corrupted beyond repair.

    Afterwards, we headed towards El Monasterio de San Francisco, the jewel of colonial Lima. At first when we made our video recording, we mistook it for something else (Iglesia de Santo Domingo). Lulu volunteered to act as our guide in front of the camera and read the Chinese description verbatim from his traveller's guide. We joined an English tour and unfortunately were stuck with a man from Alabama and his family. He made unceasing attempts to show off his knowledge of the monastery and the Bible, rudely cutting off the guide on countless occasions by basically repeating what had already been explained. Well done, Ms Granger. Five points for Gryffindor. My guess was that he was either trying to impress his family, or us. If it was the latter, he was achieving only the opposite.

The monastery has such a large collection of paintings and sculptures that it would take days to give even a brief description of a few. And it would also be unfair to their creators to have their masterpieces introduced to the public by someone with no professional knowledge; therefore I can only encourage readers to consult reliable sources or to see for themselves to satisfy their curiosity.

There was one painting that truly made an impression on me, "The Last Supper", by a Flemish Jesuit priest, dated 1697. I hate to give a superficial description, but I will try my best to describe what I saw with my eyes. It is different from The Last Supper most people are familiar with, the one by Leonardo da Vinci. Jesus and the twelve apostles sit at a table around which many little boys are serving food. Similar to da Vinci's work, a very feminine face is leaning towards Jesus. When I asked half-jokingly if "she" was Mary Magdalene, the guide insisted that he was John. Judas sits three seats to the left of Jesus and can be recognized by a devil standing right behind him. In the left corner, there are two men who are significantly smaller than the other figures. There must be a name for such a drawing style. That is the best I can do.

Eventually we got bored and began asking stupid questions with a straight face. I thought about asking if the Last Supper was a painting or a photograph, but that would have been too silly. Justin asked if Goliath was in that painting, but unfortunately the guide wasn't too familiar with that name and so that didn't work either.

Photography was prohibited inside the monastery but Lulu and Pierre believed that rules were made to be broken. Lulu did so in a secretive manner behind our shoulders. Classroom paparazzi have been his training ground. Lam Ying Pierre, however, adopted a less subtle approach. While we were learning attentively about monastic community life, a flash of lightning illuminated the room. Knowing that it wasn't raining, we immediately turned our heads to Pierre, sending a hostile message with our eyes, beaming, "You moron". I felt obliged to make a sincere apology for the immature behavior of our party and so I explained to the guide that my friend didn't understand English. Pierre's punishment was not to utter a word or to show comprehension of anything in English for the rest of the tour.

There were several courtyards inside these monasteries, the size depending on the importance of the saint. On walls that surrounded these courtyards were giant paintings with intricate details. Many heads or other body parts were missing from the rest of the pictures. The black market probably pays well for them. Although I despise people who indifferently mar the artistic value of artwork for personal benefit, I tried to convince myself that these deeds were done under the most desperate circumstances. After all, Peru is a relatively poor country. If a dead painting can save lives, the sacrifice is well worthwhile. Besides, thinking about it from the artist's perspective, I suppose nothing is more satisfying than creating works that carry weight in life and death situations. And I believe that the artists will receive their ultimate rewards in the afterlife. Nonetheless, it is also possible that these thefts were crimes of a sheerly malicious nature initiated by hatred of the Church. If that is the case, I am in no position to comment.

I never really explained why we had mistaken the monastery for something else. Having a slight recollection of Lulu's commentary, Justin asked, "Didn't you mention that this monastery was founded by a black saint? How come he is white in this painting?"

"Err . . . actually we are in a different place. This is St. Francisco," Lulu replied, embarrassing us.

We went down to the crypt where rested thousands of men, who can now be recognized only as a collection of bones.

Gerald Yeung, Wannabe Backpackers

Interestingly, they were arranged in the most organized manner: ribs with ribs, skulls with skulls. There was not a single complete skeleton sitting in a corner. This would have been unnecessarily intimidating. Surprisingly, none of us suggested a bet on staying in the dungeon overnight. If the potential risks entailed turning insane, no reward would be enough. Spending a night with the remains and spirits of a thousand people should always be avoided if possible.

What I really enjoyed in South America was the attention. Everyone on the street looked admiringly at us wherever we went, whether because they had never seen Asians or because we were simply charming. I don't know about the others but in my case it was definitely the latter. Some girls even whistled at us. This was where I belonged. Not many people are bold enough to say this, but this was the closest I felt to being David Beckham.

Many people label South America as a paradise of crime that breeds men of short temper. That could not be further away from the truth. People here were very friendly and I felt perfectly comfortable walking around. A few schoolgirls even requested a photo with us and of course we were more than happy to comply. Although Herman Melville called Lima "the saddest city on earth," I have to disagree. The decayed colonial grandeur and the cloudy winter sky certainly support his claim. The city itself may look old and perished, but what defines a city is its people. Everywhere we went, we saw people contentedly engaging in their daily obligations. Life is not easy for most of them, but they allowed no-one to see any sign of their worries.

That night, we went on a bar crawl in Barranco, a street surrounded by bars and discos on both sides. For those unfamiliar with self-destructive activities, a bar crawl is going to bar after bar until only one person is left standing. It is the most fun way to commit suicide. We basically started at one end of the Barranco and went into every other bar. In each we finished a pitcher of beer. This was what we young people have the luxury of doing.

Gerald Yeung, Wannabe Backpackers

Lulu wasn't feeling well and so we called it a day early.

Happy at Plaza Mayor, Lima, Peru.
(L to R) Gerald, Justin, Pierre (front), Brian, Lulu.

Gerald Yeung, Wannabe Backpackers

11th June
Cloudy
Lima

La Rosa Nautica
Walking with a friend in the dark is better than walking alone in the light.—Helen Keller

I woke up at 8am to watch Holland against Serbia and Montenegro. Robben scored the winner.

At 12 noon, a quick bite at a restaurant turned out to be not so quick so we basically saw the entire Mexico versus Iran game, in which O. Bravo netted twice in the three-to-one victory. With no time to lose, we hauled ass to Huacu Pucllana, a pyramid standing in the middle of a residential area. It wasn't particularly interesting except for the fact that we took obscene pictures that reenacted the daily life of the Incas, namely the mundane tasks of all humans.

We fled when Justin destroyed the steps while descending down a secret entrance to the interior of the pyramid that didn't exist. We then went to Museo de Antropologia, Arqueologia y Historia, which sucked. I never enjoy pottery exhibitions. The only exhibits worth mentioning were clay sculptures depicting different reproductive positions. Why could South Americans openly praise the divine mission of human beings in various forms of art while we conservative Chinese try so hard to avoid the subject?

The Museo de la Nacion is an amazing giant structure. It is the tallest building in its immediate neighborhood and, as one approaches, the building gets bigger. This is probably some sort of architectural feature having to do with the incline or something similar. Its interior, however, hardly lives up to its reputation. Although the building looked to be twenty stories high from the outside, it had only three floors, all displaying 10th grade artwork.

Gerald Yeung, Wannabe Backpackers

Finally, the Museo de Oro was worth every penny of the $30 entrance fee. The first level was an arsenal, filled with every kind of instrument men have invented to kill each other. On the defensive end, it also featured a collection of armour and weapons from every culture. All kinds of guns, swords, horseshoes, samurai swords and armour, spears, explosives... you name it. The whole time we were there, we had a fun discussion of how we were going to break in to the museum that night and fight each other with all the weapons on display. After we were done chopping off each other's limbs and poking each other's eyes out with ninja shuriken, we would have hot pot. It would be a lot of fun, except no-one was willing to go to the market to buy ingredients for the hot pot so we might as well call off the fight too.

Contrary to the first-floor exhibits of how to cause bloodshed, the basement sang the elegance of gold ornaments. If you ask me, all the exhibits looked weird and for a second I thought it was an exhibition of, "The Worst Ways to Waste Gold." One thing we saw was a gold disk attached to a thick round rod in the middle. Upon inspection, it was probably an ornament for the ear that was held in place by sticking the thick rod in the ear. Maybe it looked good to them, but unless the Incas had a completely different anatomy from us, it could not possibly have felt good. They definitely sacrificed too much for beauty.

We went to La Rosa Nautica for dinner, a very famous seafood restaurant. It stands at the end of a pier about fifty yards offshore. As gay as this may sound, the ambience was so romantic that if I were to take a girl there, she would not think twice about marrying me. Come to think of it, who would? The restaurant immediately reminded me of the Lighthouse of Alexandria, one of the seven wonders of the ancient world, for it lit up the shoreline like a castle on the sea, while retaining the tranquility that concealed the depth of the Pacific Ocean beyond La Costa Verde.

Gerald Yeung, Wannabe Backpackers

We ordered a bottle of Argentinean white wine to go with the best meal in Peru thus far. We had grown up throughout the course of the day: from reckless teenagers who showed little self-respect at the pyramid, to young men engaging in meaningful yet vivid conversations while enjoying good food and wine. Throughout dinner, we recounted our days in primary school, trying to remember all the names and faces with whom we had spent six years of our childhood. We began thinking about teachers, rumours, and all the things that had happened in that small school in MacDonnell Road. Moments like this remind me that making friends is a blessing.

At times, I was so engaged that I forgot about being on vacation in Peru. We were all too caught up in the moment. Looking back into the past, we grew up through recollecting our childhood thoughts from a different perspective and regretting how our childlike minds had been concealed by the practicality of the cruel world.

When I finally returned to the present from memory lane, I was glad to find myself still accompanied by the faces of those who have written countless chapters of my fondest memories.

Statue of Pachacutec. Cusco, Peru.
Photo by Pierre.

Gerald Yeung, Wannabe Backpackers

12th June
Sunny
Lima to Cusco

The Sunniest Place on Earth
The vision of this Cusco emerges mournfully from the fortress destroyed by the stupidity of illiterate Spanish conquistadors, from the violated ruins of the temples, from the sacked palaces, from the faces of a brutalized race. This is the Cusco inviting you to become a warrior and to defend, club in hand, the freedom and the life of the Inca.—Ernesto Che Guevara

Lulu and I woke up at 7am to get his visa. His fate will be decided when we next return to Lima from Cusco. At a bank nearby, we exchanged more *soles*, the Peruvian currency, and found out that we had been badly ripped off at Los Angeles airport. Then, we went to a McDonald's that didn't have fries. McDonald's without fries is like playing soccer without a ball. Lulu had his photo taken with the girl who worked there. Girls in Peru were not drop dead gorgeous, but their perpetual smiles held the secrets to their charm.

After a short flight to Cusco, we were sucked into a mini drama. Two groups of travel agents fought over us. One was from the agency we booked the hotel with and the other was the one we met at Lima airport. During the verbal attacks, Lulu was lying down by the baggage carrier, suffering from altitude sickness. We finally decided to stick with the original agent and Lulu slowly came back to life.

A metropolitan city built in a rural environment, Cusco possesses an irresistible charm. Similar to Lima, Cusco has inherited much European culture, especially in Plaza de Armas and El Catedral, which have become "living" evidence of the colonial era. The Incas, the people of the Sun, obviously worshipped Inti, the sun god. One can find statues and monuments embedding symbolisms of the Sun all around. The Incas certainly picked a good site to build their city, as Cusco, a city of 3500m altitude, has the highest UV level on Earth,[1] which brought them closer to the sun than anywhere else. The name "Cusco" means the navel of the world, which refers to Tahuantinsuyo, the Inca world. Insightful individuals see a different side of Cusco. "The vision of this Cusco emerges mournfully from the fortress destroyed by the stupidity of illiterate Spanish conquistadors, from the violated ruins of the temples, from the sacked palaces, from the faces of a brutalized race. This is the Cusco inviting you to become a warrior and to defend, club in hand, the freedom and the life of the Inca."[2] I found that description extremely fortifying; I am ready to kill someone now.

That night, we visited the biggest local market in a warehouse and purchased T-shirts, baby alpaca scarves, ponchos and many souvenirs.

Ollyantas train station, Peru.
Photo by Louis.

Gerald Yeung, Wannabe Backpackers

13th June
Sunny
Cusco to Aguas Calientes, Machu Picchu

The Lost City
Machu Picchu es un viaje a la serenidad del alma, a la eternal fusion con el cosmos, alli sentimos nuestra fragilidad. Es una de las maravillas más grandes de Sudamérica. Un reposar de mariposas en el epicentro del gran circulo de la vida. Otro milagro más.—Pablo Neruda

Machu Picchu is a trip to the serenity of the soul, to eternal fusion with the cosmos, there we feel our own fragility. It is one of the greatest marvels of South America. A resting place of butterflies at the epicentre of the great circle of life. One more miracle.— Pablo Neruda

This was the day I would never forget. Visiting Machu Picchu was a spiritual and intellectual experience. For me in particular it held special significance because I have wanted to go there ever since I learned about it, and I consider it one of the places a man must see.

We woke up at 5.45am, packed light and went to the bus-station. Pierre, whom we had nicknamed DJ Tree,[3] dressed up as an Inca boy by wearing his new Peruvian poncho for the occasion. The bus ride was bearable, but the last hour wasn't particularly fun for me because I thought I had lost the train tickets. I was relieved in the end when Brian told me he had them.

Brian and I got stuck at Ollyantas for an hour and a half due to the poor arrangements of the travel agent whom we began to despise. The wait wasn't bad though because these three girls were staring at us (like every girl does) and I took the initiative of a gentleman to approach them. One of them with an Inca look was quite cute. She was from Cusco and she seemed nice and quiet.

Gerald Yeung, Wannabe Backpackers

Her name was Patty. Unfortunately, I could hardly unleash my smoothness on her because another girl, who happened to be her half-sister, spoke good English and wouldn't shut up. As a form of revenge, I deliberately didn't remember her name and I stared at Patty the whole time. The only thing I got out of the conversation was a cocktail called Machu Picchu and that we should never mix the three layers together. Eventually, we grew sick of talking so we decided to watch the World Cup instead. It was South Korea against Togo. The Asians came back with a two-to-one victory, but their attitude was pathetic. They were given a free kick well within shooting range but they kicked it back to the keeper for possession. Togo was terrible too. How did they make the World Cup? They were playing like they didn't care about the outcome, as they had no intention to attack even after Korea took the lead. Games like this make me think that the World Cup isn't as exciting any more.

    The train ride was very enjoyable. As soon as we got out of the station, we caught a clear view of the mountain range. Hanaqpacha Inn was located along the railroad dedicated to *Hiram Bingham*, the luxurious train that brings tourists from all over Peru to Aguas Calientes, named after the explorer who rediscovered Machu Picchu. Before departing for the ruins, I had to deal with the US embassy for half an hour, which was less than pleasant.

    The bus took us up to the ruins by means of a zigzag road.

    We hired a guide who turned out to be quite a character. At first I hated him because he wouldn't shut up and his voice bugged me. Therefore I didn't bother to commit his name to memory because I decided that he deserved no better treatment than the girl who prevented me from meeting the Inca love of my life. But soon I took a liking to him because he talked in a musical manner. He reminded me of Ali G.

    Machu Picchu was built around 1,460 AD during the Inca expansion, on Urubamba Valley 2,430m above sea level. [4]

Although it was forgotten by the world until Hiram Bingham rediscovered it in 1911, locals never abandoned it during all those years. "Archeological evidence shows that Machu Picchu was not a conventional city, but a country retreat for Inca nobility."[5] Even in the eyes of modern billionaires, Machu Picchu is quite a lot of work for just a holiday resort.

It is believed that the Incas chose this site for a particular reason—behind Machu Picchu lies a mountain range that resembles an Inca face looking up to the sky, with Huayna Picchu as the nose. After seeing the real thing, I understood that the postcards did not exaggerate. The first sight of Machu Picchu left us speechless—we were looking for adjectives to describe what was unveiled before us. If it leaves us modern men in amazement, I can hardly imagine the magnitude of the miracle it was five hundred years ago. Resting on a mountain ridge that overlooks the Urubamba valley, Machu Picchu provides a serene environment that invites its visitors to nirvana.

Unfortunately, men strive to prevent anything from being perfect. Machu Picchu's natural charisma has been marred by the country's exceedingly zealous tourism. This consequence of modernization pollutes its sacred ambience and spoils the spiritual experience for those who have the utmost respect for the Incas. In fact, the government is planning on constructing cable cars so that Machu Picchu can be even more accessible. This thought disgusts me. Is it an attempt to turn the sacred remains of their ancestors into an amusement park for profit? Although the government indirectly regulates tourism by making everything very expensive, they need to do better if they are to prevent the ruins from being demolished by their own hand. Some may argue that the Incas left Machu Picchu as an inexhaustible source of fortune for their descendants. If that were the case, they would make amazing businessmen nowadays. Nonetheless, only qualified persons should see Machu Picchu, namely, those who arrive by the Inca Trail. By taking the same steps as laid down by the Incas, one would be able to understand the prominence of the monument by experiencing the hardship its creators endured. Well, I am in no position to comment because I took the train. But before I die, I will do the Inca Trail. This is a vow.

We had French-Peruvian cuisine at Indi Feliz. It was a very homey restaurant that served us a satisfying meal. Afterwards, some looked for Internet access while others had a few drinks. Travelling around Aguas Calientes was a physical challenge as all the streets rested on steep inclines, and the city's 3338-metre altitude was not helping. Justin and I intended to walk all the way up the hill to look for the best bar, but we gave up after a minute. We sat down at the nearest one to catch our breath.

We retired to our rooms and played Big2 for the rest of the evening. Our game was interrupted by an untimely call from Maria who told us that we would have to wait at the bus-station for three hours for our pickup. I told her that such a poor arrangement was unacceptable by any standard and I insisted that I would neither wait nor pay extra to go back to Cusco as soon as I stepped out of the train. Sometimes we need to take a firm stance and throw the ball to the other side of the court for them to deal with. I guess the volleyball court teaches you more than just how to take a hit in the face. Maria hung up to set things straight while I got back to the card game.

Feasting llamas at Macchu Pichu, Peru.
Photo by Justin.

Five Guardian Angels of Machu Picchu.
(L to R) Pierre, Gerald, Lulu, Justin, Brian.

Before the sacred place. Photo by Lulu.
(L to R) Gerald, our guide, Justin, Brian, Pierre.
Machu Picchu, Peru.

Gerald Yeung, Wannabe Backpackers

14th June
Partly sunny
Aguas Calientes to Cusco

Corpus Christi
A timid person is frightened before a danger, a coward during the time, and a courageous person afterward.—Jean Paul Richter

Pierre woke me up to deal with the call from Maria. It was five to eight. She basically told me that everything was fine. A car would be waiting for us at Ollyantas as soon as we stepped out of the train and we wouldn't have to pay a penny more. My strategy did work. I have had it used on me many times and finally I knew what it feels like to be a bitch—good. What I didn't understand was why she had to repeat such a simple fact five times, exactly four times too many. By the time she was ready to shut up, I was wide-awake and quite annoyed. I turned on the TV and saw Spain crush Ukraine four-nil, goals from Xabi Alonso, Fernando Torres and two from David Villa. The Spanish seemed to be worthy contenders. Afterwards, we had a really shitty breakfast in the lobby. Then, Lulu and I stayed to make flight changes for his visa appointment. By the time we were done, the other three were nowhere to be found. We later found out that they went to the hot spring.

So Lulu and I went shopping to kill time. I bought a pair of green pajamas pants for fifteen *soles* after bargaining like a bitch. Saving two *soles* (less than one US dollar) meant nothing, but flirting with the girl was priceless. I lied to her that I was completely broke, which was only ninety soles away from the truth. When we had a deal, I recommended that she should have her photograph taken with me so that I could advertise her business. Gerald scored again. She wanted a copy and I promised her one when I come back ten years from now.

In Aguas Calientes (and basically every city we went),

Gerald Yeung, Wannabe Backpackers

people assumed that we were Japanese and greeted us with "Konichiwa" all the time. First of all, I am not Japanese. Even if I was, I would still be annoyed if people defeated the purpose of my vacation by constantly reminding me of my origins while I was making an attempt to retreat from my culture.

We found the lost party at a decent restaurant where we all had lunch. They smelled like copper from the hot spring. I wondered if they could conduct electricity. I ordered Ceviche, my favorite Peruvian dish composed of chunks of raw fish with onion in marinade. The marinade used was typically citrus-based, limes and lemons being the most common fruit used. Although Ceviche originated in Peru, it has gained popularity throughout South America. Nowadays, many Latin American countries have given Ceviche a flavor of individuality to suit their tastes. For example, Ceviche always goes with chips or popcorn in Ecuador.

The train-ride back took only an hour and it was very relaxing. I fell deeply asleep under the sun and gentle breeze. Adding to the pleasant experience, I was lucky enough to sit across from a really cute blonde British girl. Even though she was a little fat (actually quite fat), I still found her attractive. That isn't good, is it? Although I liked the chubby girl, I didn't think so highly of her friends for they smelt awful. Being backpackers does not give them the privilege not to shower. I respected their personal choice of life but why did others have to suffer? Besides, personal hygiene is an indication of self-respect. How do you expect others to respect you when you don't even respect yourself?

When we arrived at Ollyantas, we got in the car that Maria had reminded me five times about. There was no way the four of us could last two hours in the back seat so I volunteered to ride in the trunk, which was a lot better than everyone reckoned. The driver was hauling as much ass the whole way, passing car after car, as if he was being chased by cops (which you will soon find not at all far-fetched). Most of us were worried, especially Lulu in the front seat. I, however, enjoyed flying along the country roads.

Gerald Yeung, Wannabe Backpackers

We stopped to take pictures of the snow mountain, then we stopped again to see a person attempting a bungee jump. Within minutes, a crowd of at least twenty people built up by the road to anticipate him flying in mid air, or a giant splash of blood if we were lucky. After five long minutes, he decided to chicken out. Our driver honked at him as I yelled "pussy." It was a prime time to make an enemy because by the time he reached the ground to come over and punch me, we were well gone.

Eventually we arrived at Cusco but we were pulled over twice before getting off the vehicle. I didn't understand what the cops were saying to the driver but he was given a ticket because of an amigo in the trunk, which would be me. He tried to convince me to pay a hundred *soles* to compensate for his loss, but I insisted that I was not at fault, given that I had asked for his permission in advance. I suggested that he should talk to Maria but I never knew what happened to him in the end.

As soon as we arrived, Lulu and I went to the LAN Peru office to change our original 11.15am flight to the 7.50am flight back to Lima. I thought about implementing the change for all of us just to make everyone's life harder, but my conscience stopped me. Later on, I still lied to them that I had and the truth was not revealed until after they had reset their alarm clocks. And of course, I was badly beaten up.

Today was a big local holiday, Corpus Christi. Sixty days after Easter Sunday, fifteen saints and virgins from different places come to the cathedral in Cusco to salute the body of Christ. The parade started at around noon in Plaza de Armas. Although we missed out on most of the celebration, we could still detect a festival mood throughout the city from the singing and dancing that didn't cease until sunset. The receptionist at the hotel reminded us to be extra careful with our belongings and recommended against going outside if possible. As if we were going to listen to her! Any experienced pickpocket would know better than to rob five tough men. Besides, there were a lot of cops around to prevent anyone from ruining the party. We went to a grill restaurant and ordered a giant platter that included a pork chop, half a chicken, inedible steak, blood sausage and cow heart. The three giant plates of fries, which came with the platter, were left intact. It was the sacrifice we had to make to look good. In case you haven't already noticed, we were all about appearance.

El Catedral, Cusco, Peru.
Photo By Louis.

Gerald Yeung, Wannabe Backpackers

15th June
Cloudy
Cusco to Lima

Bar Crawl Two
Beer is proof that God loves us and wants us to be happy.
   —Benjamin Franklin

Lulu and I woke up at the first break of daylight to go to the airport. When we arrived at Lima, we got into a taxi with a driver called Jesús. The name sounded familiar but I couldn't remember where I had heard it before. It was about time to give myself a Spanish name so I introduced myself as Gerardo. We got to watch an hour of England vs. Trinidad & Tobago game at the hotel before heading over to the US embassy. We missed both goals from Crouch and Gerard in the last ten minutes.

We were told at the door that Lulu had to go in alone. I wonder what they were going to make him do this time. With very limited options, I waited for him at McDonald's, where I spent three and a half hours reading, writing postcards and breathing in the odour of fried food. It felt like eternity and if I hadn't promised Lulu's mother that I would take good care of her precious son, I really would simply have left. Eventually Lulu showed up with his new visa and we were relieved that the curse was finally lifted. This passport saga made Lulu and me grow a lot closer to each other. I also learnt what it feels like to be a refugee, without suffering the experience myself.

Taxis in Peru don't run on meters; the fare is negotiable. There are two kinds of taxi: licensed and unlicensed. At first when we were still cautious about safety, we would only take licensed ones even though they charged twice as much, but we soon started picking only the cheaper ones since we could hardly tell the difference. Although we made the habit of negotiating, I think we were still overcharged on numerous occasions.

Gerald Yeung, Wannabe Backpackers

The rest of the afternoon was uneventful. That night, we went to a Peruvian restaurant called Las Tejas. It was our last night in Lima, and we were going to make it memorable. First, we revisited Atlantic City and poured our parents' hard-earned money into the roulette pool. We were evidently gamblers in the making. No-one ended up winning this time but we managed to entertain ourselves for an hour.

It was 11pm and our flight would depart in just over eight hours. It would be logical to go back and have a good night's sleep. Well, if that thought ever crossed your mind, you should never go on vacation with us. We were not leaving Lima without visiting Barranco once more. We put on our game face and drained five pitchers of domestic beer. Later on we each tried a Machu Picchu, a cocktail named after the famous ancient city, just in case you weren't paying attention earlier. It consists of three layers—some red fruit juice at the bottom, yellow mango juice in the middle, and a straight shot of pisco on top. I took the advice of that girl and didn't stir the drink. Using a straw, we started from the bottom, which was heavenly. The pleasant experience ended at the first taste of hard alcohol. Not determined enough to continue, we started looking around and found each other leaving a dark green layer of death in the glass. On a second thought, Machu Picchu taught us a very important lesson of life: we sip the sweet fruit juice merrily, hardly knowing that death is waiting for us at the very end of the flower tunnel; only the strongest survives. Justin tried to be the superman and downed the drink in one gulp. He ended up vomiting half of it back into the glass. There is a fine line between heroics and stupidity, and it takes no more than the wit of a First-Grader to figure out to which side Justin belongs.

We went dancing in a discoteca for a little bit until we headed back to McDonald's for food. We were all too drunk to function and somehow Brian, DJ Tree and I forgot about the food we ordered and just went back to the hotel room. Lulu and Justin came back half an hour later to brag about an act of philanthropy. Not knowing what to do with Brian's fries, they wanted to give them away to children on the street. But instead of accepting the generous offer, the children pointed at the hamburger in Justin's hand. Apparently the phrase, "Beggars can't be choosers", doesn't exist in Spanish.

Machu Picchu, the drink.
(L to R) Lulu, Justin, Pierre, Gerald, Brian.
Barranco, Lima, Peru.

Gerald Yeung, Wannabe Backpackers

16th June
Cloudy
Lima to Buenos Aires

Home Alone

"Howdy do. This is Peter McCallister, the father. I'd like a hotel room please, with an extra large bed, a TV, and one of those little refrigerators you have to open with a key. Credit card? You got it."—Kevin McCallister, *Home Alone 2: Lost in New York*

Our flight to Buenos Aires departed at 7.15am, which required us to leave the hotel by 4.30, yet we still decided to party until 2am. I am defending myself by blaming this on the irresponsible nature of adolescence. But we didn't get away unpunished. Everyone looked like a zombie in the morning and would have traded the entire world for extra sleep.

We arrived at the airport on time despite the terrible shape we were in. They scanned my duffle bag and asked to check the contents of my lotion. They actually smelt it, examined it, and even applied it to their skins for inspection. I wasn't too pleased but I guess somebody could have used it to disguise a chemical weapon.

I suffered a similar fate at the carry-on scan. This time the victim was my wallet. They found this big dollar coin, a gift from my aunt that I kept as a lucky charm. They stared at it skeptically and I could read their eyes saying, "I thought Americans made dollar bills." But they were not giving up until they proved me a terrorist. In fact, they were willing to settle for interrogating me about any item out of the ordinary. So when they discovered the secret compartment and threw me a dirty look, I knew immediately what was coming. Now what should I say about the hidden condom? Well, this item was not kept as a lucky charm: it has been in my wallet for the past two years and unfortunately, it inevitably reflected how cool I am socially. It has probably

Gerald Yeung, Wannabe Backpackers

expired anyway and most men would find the implication devastating. But it was no time to mourn; the battle was far from over. Being the only person who knew the truth, I had the cards to play the situation to my advantage. I was like "Yeah! What can I say? I am a player, a pimp." Did they understand English? That was not important. My intended audience was my four cute little friends. This is how men move up the hierarchy. The deception will end the moment they read this journal. Whatever, a temporary victory is a victory. The security guy could not help laughing and the security girl covered her face for a very long time to conceal her embarrassment. I retrieved my belongings and walked away like a champion. A battle well fought. Thank God I was not travelling with my parents, or worse still, my grandparents. Half an hour later, we passed out on the plane so I can't really tell you what happened.

We arrived at Buenos Aires, the capital of Argentina. We got into a taxi that took us through the city to the five-star Marriott Plaza Hotel. Plaza San Martin was built in 1909. About ten years ago, the Marriott chain built a hotel with modern facilities on an antiquated site there. They certainly did a good job sticking with the antique theme. For example, all the hotel staff looked like Alfred, Batman's butler. The Marriott dressed them in tuxedos and carefully parted their hair. In contrast, our clothes had been worn repeatedly and we had "hangover" written all over our faces. They stared at us as if we weren't supposed to be there. Thanks to the courtesy of a friend working for the Marriott, we were able to enjoy its luxury at an affordable rate.

In comparison to our habitation in Lima, Marriott's room was heaven, with two comfy queen-size beds and everything a decent hotel room should have. We wasted no time and went down to the pool. It was nine degrees outside, but we swam in the heated outdoor pool, played several games, took a lot of pictures, and then went inside to the sauna and Jacuzzi area. DJ Tree raised the temperature to the maximum and locked himself in the sauna room. I went inside for a minute to keep him company until I found it unexpectedly difficult to breathe.

"DJ, I can't breathe." I could barely speak in fact.

"It's because of the moisture in the air, I just poured the entire bucket," he replied at ease with his eyes closed.

"How about we stop pouring water?"

"Then your nose will start bleeding."

"OK, I'm out of here."

Every now and then, he would ask me to take pictures of him naked or having only a particularly intimate part hidden under a water bucket. DJ was not the same boy we once knew at primary school. This summer, we gained insights into his wild hobbies, the content of which would be highly inappropriate to be shared here. One time when we had to take a huge grown-up decision, he asked that we take a picture of the five of us naked to enhance unity. No-one spoke for a whole minute before I broke the silence and said, "I don't see how these two things are related." We had the suspicion that he was just finding an excuse to see how handsome we were without our clothes. The subject was never brought up again and we pretended as if it had never happened. . . . Our friendship survived yet another challenge.

Buenos Aires is also known as "The Paris of the South" and I could easily see the connection. The buildings and the streets were heavily influenced by European culture while retaining a unique Latino charm. Buenos Aires is a cosmopolitan city without the rundown districts and dirty streets associated with other big cities.

For dinner, we went to a steak restaurant nearby, recommended by Lulu's traveller's guide. After dinner Brian decided to stay in while the rest of us went to a bar called Sahara in Recoleta. It was a big bar-restaurant where all the staff were dressed as safari rangers. Judging from the Marriott Plaza Alfreds and these rangers, it seemed that Argentinians know how to throw costume parties. There was a band playing and the general atmosphere was lively except that it was more suitable for older people.

Synchronized swimming. Photo by Pierre.
Marriott Plaza Hotel, Buenos Aires, Argentina.
(L to R) Gerald, Brian, Justin.

Plaza de los Dos Congresos Parlament. Photo by Louis.
Buenos Aires, Argentina.

Gerald Yeung, Wannabe Backpackers

17th June
Cloudy
Buenos Aires

Shampoo
I met my wife by breaking two of my rules: never date a girl seriously that you meet at a nightclub and never date a fan.
—Corey Feldman

The last time we slept so well must have been in Hong Kong. We woke up satisfactorily at 11am, just in time to catch the second half of Portugal vs. Iran. Portugal won with a stunner from Deco and a penalty by Ronaldo. After a quick bite, we walked towards Plaza de Mayo through Avenida Florida, which was not the most efficient route because we fell into the temptations offered by the flanking shops every five seconds. At a rate of one tenth of a mile an hour, we finally arrived at Plaza de Mayo after walking for two hours.

There was some sort of religious service going on and we tried our best not to interrupt the ceremony. Besides being the destination of Sunday Christian pilgrimage, the Plaza is also the permanent home for pigeons that have become accustomed to humans. Lulu bought two packs of pigeon treats and we did some pigeon feeding, as gay as that sounds. Justin tried to pour some treats on my head but I found out before the birds started crowding up on me.

After the birds were fed, we needed to feed ourselves and to watch Italy's game. As an Italian fan, I endured ninety minutes of frustration. Gilardino scored but the advantage was soon cancelled out by Zaccardo's own goal. Three players were sent off (De Rossi, Pope and some American guy). To calm our minds, we drank Quilmes, the most popular local beer, and finally understood how it became the "official" beer of the city.

We saw the Obelisk of Buenos Aires, built in 1936 to

commemorate the 400th anniversary of the founding of the city. It was situated in the centre of Plaza de la Républica, at the intersection of Avenida Corrientes and Nueve de Julio, one of the widest avenues in the world, named after Argentine Independence Day (9 July 1816). A renowned opera house with an international reputation, Teatro Colón carries an international reputation worth fifteen blocks of walking. Yet we found out only at the door that we were allowed to take pictures only outside.

After copious walking, our legs had done enough work for the day; and we decided that it was time for the heart to work. So we took a taxi to Puerto Madero to visit The Casino Buenos Aires, the largest casino in town, located on two Mississippi-style boats. We went through a scrupulous scan at the entrance and had to leave our cell-phones and bags at the storage—it was no amateur hour. At first, we had intended to visit a casino more similar to an arcade where we could do whatever we wanted, but we had obviously knocked at the wrong door. The minimum bet at every table was five pesos, which prevented us from randomly throwing down chips. I had come all that way so I thought I might as well play.

Not knowing too much about roulette, I decided to go all in and threw fifty pesos on red. Justin did the same thing and we combined to make a generous donation to the owner of the casino who could now get even more women. Brian adopted our strategy and won a hundred pesos. After five very exciting minutes, our hearts had had their workouts for the night. Justin and I took a losers' picture together outside our boat. Not being able to find a taxi that would illegally take five passengers, we had to walk out of the pier. On second thoughts, walking home from the casino was bad luck.

We patronized an appealing restaurant that displayed a giant, powerful grill. Appearance is often deceiving. Let me begin with the service: the waiter yelled at us for not understanding Spanish. Perhaps that explained why he had to work in a restaurant. As a civilized gentleman, I sincerely apologized for not speaking every single language in the world fluently. When we were done with their shitty food, it took them forty-five minutes to give us the bill. We left without leaving a tip, which would have happened anyway to make up for the loss at the casino.

We went back to the hotel gym to exercise before more unhealthy late night activities. It was fun until the guy in charge insisted on showing us special drills. He took every opportunity to stick his ass out, which made me a little uncomfortable. Judging from his physique (short but very strong) and his voice (flamboyantly gay), I think his motif could not be more obvious.

Finally, it was time to experience the nightlife of Buenos Aires. Knowing that fifty-year-old Alfreds had little clubbing information to offer, we needed to consult other sources. We began at a pub nearby, where a waiter called Marti gave us info on the best places to go at night. In Buenos Aires, nightclubs send people to give out flyers on the street. It is very common here and they do it in broad daylight. Marti saw one of these cards and described the club in broken English.

"Dollars, good. Pesos, not as good."
I guess he was trying to tell us to use US dollars there. Then he got excited as he explained their service.

"Fifty dollars" (he started dancing); "A hundred dollars" (he lay down like a king).

We got a rough idea but we were not planning to go unless we couldn't find any good discos. Subconsciously, we were still uncomfortable with going to a nightclub.

Despite the acting and dancing that were not required by his waiter's contract, we only gave him change for tips, which he wasn't too happy about. Whatever. So far, we had been paying minimal to no tips, partly because we were students, partly because we would never go back to the same restaurant/bar again, and mostly because we were cheap. Cry about it.

Gerald Yeung, Wannabe Backpackers

    We took a taxi to Asia de Cuba, a club near Dock Number One, recommended by Marti. It looked very classy but we were denied admission because they were throwing a private party. Not knowing what we should do, we wandered around the dock and took pictures of the Women's Bridge at Puerto Madero.
    Eventually three girls walked by and we were not letting them go until we had gathered enough intelligence. The one I was carrying on a conversation with was Dañela. She was a little chubby, but I thought she was cute. Again, that doesn't sound good, does it? She was being really helpful by telling me where to go, etc. At some point, the objective changed.
    I didn't care if we weren't going anywhere; I just hoped that the conversation would never end. The girls left after giving us ample advice, but I was glad that they came back immediately. Leaving us is never easy. Dañela came back to tell us about parks with girls walking around ready to be picked up. (She did this gesture with her hand that I didn't understand.) I had to make several guesses in my head before saying, "prostitutes"? Dañela went, "Yeah, yeah." I laughed and told her that we weren't interested, but I would write that down just in case. I saw DJ putting a big X on the map.
    We got into a taxi and the driver said he would take us to the coolest club in town. We didn't realize that he was talking about a nightclub until we arrived. At first we told him that it was not our cup of tea, but he encouraged us to just take a look and see if we liked it. Knowing that the club was paying for our taxi fare, we felt obliged to at least check it out. We sent DJ Tree in as a scout and he returned with an executive summary decent enough to convince us all to go in. It was a bad choice: pole dancing was stupid, some of the girls were pretty hot, but they were hitting on older men the whole time, figuring that they had more resources to offer. Sending DJ as a scout was doomed to be a mistake because he would sell his soul to naked women. We basically sat there for half an hour but Brian's eyes never left the

lesbian porno on TV.

    The club paid for our ride there, and it would be logical for them to do the same for our ride home; that was our assumption. As soon as we got out of the taxi, I heard Justin saying, "Run, run". Without figuring out what was happening, we ran upstairs as fast as we could but still looked as composed as possible. We took the stairs instead of the elevator. After we got to the second floor, Justin explained that the driver was yelling at him as he was closing the door. Something definitely made him a little upset; it most likely had to do with the fare. Just when we were about to enter our room, Batman's butler came and told us to pay the taxi guy at the lobby. Damn it, we were so close. It looked like we had no choice but to pay him. But before we did so, we accused the driver for sending us the wrong message by not starting the meter. A couple of younger Alfreds helped out in the verbal bombardment.

    "Where did you come from?" young Alfred asked just out of curiosity.

    "Shampoo. Haha," we replied, embarrassed.

We all burst into laughter. Judging from the fact that we were too shy to go to a nightclub, we began to acknowledge that we would never be bad people even if we tried. I am not saying that anyone who goes to a nightclub is bad, but if we were scared to simply walk into one, I would not count on us robbing banks, killing people or even beating up children.

Gerald Yeung, Wannabe Backpackers

18th June
Cloudy
Buenos Aires

Metrosexuals in the Making
Always do sober what you said you'd do drunk. That will teach you to keep your mouth shut.—Ernest Hemingway

We woke up at noon and left our rooms an hour later for lunch. I bought an Aimar Argentine jersey. It was not the official replica but I didn't care because true Argentines wear those. When in Rome. We saw half of the Brazil vs. Australia game at a café, which was possible only because of the remarkably slow service. After lunch we went to Avenida Santa Fe, a really, really long road that was supposedly the best place to shop in the city. Although most shops were closed (95% of them) on Sundays, we did come across a Dior shop where our heiresses spent two full hours and almost all their cash. They said the clothes here were ten times cheaper than those in Hong Kong; I never knew that Dior was an expensive brand. I sat down and took a nap while they entered the fitting room repeatedly. Their clothes were too dull in colour for me; I prefer bright-colour clothing to reflect my colourful life.

Buenos Aires is dead on Sunday: everything is closed and there are like five people on the street. I think it has to do with religion more than indolence. After all, more than 80% of the Argentine population is Roman Catholic. They obviously follow strictly the teachings of God, even the day He rests.

I went back to the hotel while they spent even more time and money on Dior. I hope all their purchases were fake.

Throughout this trip I learned a lot more about Ernesto "Che" Guevara, a physician who later became a symbol of socialist revolution, both from reading the *Motorcycle Diaries* and by visiting Buenos Aires. He was admired as a national hero in

Argentina, with a status equal to that of Maradona, who was virtually a God.

I make a habit of sending myself a postcard from every city so that I will remember where I have been to. I love to receive mail; it is good to know that somebody loves me. The postcard I chose for Buenos Aires to be sent to "Gerald" was one with the portrait of El Che because he best represented Buenos Aires, at least in my eyes. I admired him not for his political involvement (which I know little about), but for his sense of humour and adventurous spirit. He is a hero in many people's minds and I am bound to offend half the world if I say that we have things in common. That, however, is not enough to prevent me from pointing it out. We both took a trip around South America, even though our experiences slightly differed—he had to worry about where the next drink would be coming from while we had trouble deciding how many designer-brand jackets we should buy. In fact, DJ had already asked me that question like eight times that day.

We went to the steak restaurant again for dinner, and this time the service was noticeably worse, probably because we gave them like a two pesos tip last time.

We went back for a Jacuzzi before heading out for a drink at an Irish Pub. We tried our luck again at Asia de Cuba but we were turned down again at the door. A taxi driver brought us to a ginormous *discoteca*. As we were paying the cover charge at the door, they told Justin that two of his bills were fake. We went into a long discussion of how and where he obtained the counterfeit. Now that we took a closer look, I could have done a better job with home printers.

From what we saw in the past two nights, nightclubs seemed to be the only outlet to nightlife in Buenos Aires. Just as we were about to make such an assumption, we found the biggest disco ever. I guess this city is all about extremes.

This place was huge: it was essentially five big discos

combined. The glass windows and roof captured the night view of the beautiful docks and the designer used many water-related decorations such as pools and fountains, turning the disco into a twenty-first century creation. Unfortunately, size is not a guarantee of good parties, just like in many other things. It didn't get crowded (more like ceased being empty) until about 3am. Teenagers probably had to wait till their parents were fast asleep before they could sneak out. I asked some random girls for a drink but realized that flirting with them would be too much of a hassle—speaking Spanish against the deafening background music was asking too much of me. It would have been better if I had come with a girl. Brian was texting Tiffany the whole time, at the rate of literally a message per minute. Given that each message cost like two dollars, I could not wait till he got his phone bill. Being the introvert that he was, he never told us much about her, but I am intrigued to see what she is like. In fact, I am more interested in the recipe of her charm potion and in learning the spells she used to lock Brian's heart in the world's most secure prison. DJ Tree was wasted again after two drinks and when that happens, stupid suggestions flowed freely out of his mouth, one of them being nominating the club to be a national monument in Buenos Aires. That could get annoying sometimes, but at least somebody was having fun.

  In an environment where hitting on girls seemed too difficult, we had to entertain ourselves with our own means. We played a lot of drinking games, but none of them were too successful because we had to stop for Brian to send text messages every thirty seconds. Eventually our imagination ran out and we decided to call it a night. We had expected Buenos Aires to be the best place for parties among all our destinations, but our experience here obviously failed our expectations. Now I see why people here had to turn to nightclubs for late night entertainment. We certainly didn't make the most out of the services at Shampoo; maybe we were not old enough to understand. Walking back to the main street with my ears still drumming, I stared at the dock and the Women's Bridge for the last time in probably several years. I looked at the dark water and wondered how deep it was. Something else was troubling my mind: I needed to pee really badly. But before I did so, two things needed to go down into the dock first: Brian's cell-phone and DJ Tree.

Avenida Florida. Buenos Aires, Argentina.
Photo by Brian.

Gerald Yeung, Wannabe Backpackers

19th June
Sunny
Buenos Aires to Iguazu

Spoiled Kids vs. Hostile Girl

All charming people, I fancy, are spoiled. It is the secret of their attraction. —Oscar Wilde

8.30am wake up call. I picked up the phone and heard a woman speaking Filipino in a very soft voice. I tried to remember what had happened the previous night, but before I had any success, I fell asleep again. Half an hour later we decided that somebody should wake up but no-one volunteered. I unmistakably remembered beating Brian in rock, paper, scissors, even though my eyes were half-closed, but he denied the loss. Justin pretended to be deep asleep so he didn't even participate. I was clearly more mature than the boy still spellbound by third-grade puppy love and so I got up, hoping to teach by example. But before I successfully entered the bathroom, my evil self convinced me that Brian could not walk away unpunished. I acquiesced and smashed him with a pillow. The pillow fight started abruptly but ended just as fast when I began throwing punches with my shoe.

The lack of discipline left us very little time to pack and of course we left later than we had planned. But at times like this, those who were truly metrosexual rose to the occasion. While Brian was still in the shower, Lulu came up to tell us that he would patronize the Dior shop once more. We didn't name him Mainland Man for no reason. But when our suitcases would not close without the aid of our full body weight, we knew that we were no better.

"Home Alone" ended in a grand fashion—the scene consisted of three full-grown men carrying our bags to taxis and Batman's butlers waving us goodbye with huge, genuine smiles. The Marriott must have been glad to see us leave. I hope we didn't get blacklisted.

We checked in five minutes before boarding and departed for Iguaza. I caught up with my diary on the plane and took a nap. The next thing I remembered was seeing nothing but dense jungle. And among thousands of dark green trees stood a pink one. It was pretty, but where were the buildings? Lulu, where the hell have you brought us?

We tried to look for a better hotel because living in hostels could be tough, especially after three nights of five-star luxury. We took a look at one a cab driver recommended. The rooms were nice, but it was very small and the neighborhood was too quiet. We went back to the original plan—Hostel-Inn Iguazu. It was like a campsite with quite a few young people engaging in board games, singing in a circle and other social activities. In general, the big "club house" provided a cozy atmosphere. I wish I could say the same about the rooms. Moist sheets covered the beds. We had a private bathroom with no source of ventilation. It had a strange smell to begin with and DJ Tree's unannounced number two didn't help. These were already the best rooms they had to offer and this thought scared me. It was certainly a challenge, but we thought that we should see it as another hurdle to jump before we actually became backpackers.

After unloading our bags, we went upstairs for hamburgers and a few games of pool. While we were waiting for food, Lulu and I explored the activities the hostel provided.

"We want to do some crazy shit," I told the girl at the counter.

"Wow, you were asking for the best rooms and now you want the best things to do. We will have to work very hard for you," she replied with a sarcastic look on her face.

Oh snap. This bitch is bad news. But her condescending remarks hardly troubled me because if I couldn't deal with this girl, I wouldn't have lived till this day. Besides, I was the master of mental warfare.

"Whatever, we are spoiled. We can't help it." Thank you Paris Hilton.

Afterwards, we played some soccer. I scored so many goals that I lost count. It was fun. There was a girl called Sophia on the other team. She was the crazy type with too much energy. Others went easy on her, but I showed no sympathy for a girl and I knocked her down a few times. Cry about it. There was also a British kid who looked flamboyantly gay. Justin and others kept teasing me that he was my brother. In general, there were a lot of weirdoes in that place, ourselves included, of course.

After showering we went to the supermarket nearby, which was a grocery store the size of a hotel room. Buffet dinner was okay. I thought it was more than just edible and I gave them credit for it being healthy. We played cards, watched stars and went to sleep.

To the jungle. Iguazu, Argentina.
Louis, Gerald, Pierre, Justin, Brian.
(3rd & 2nd passenger seats of jeep, L to R)

Gerald Yeung, Wannabe Backpackers

20th June
Cloudy
Iguazu

A First Taste of the Waterfall

Let us keep the dance of rain our fathers kept and tread our dreams beneath the jungle sky.—Arna Bontemps

We woke up at 7am for a really shitty breakfast (literally nothing to eat but bread) and went on our excursion. We got into a roofless Jeep and everyone immediately regretted not wearing long sleeves, except for Lulu who was always well prepared. After about half an hour of driving, we got off and began the hike. I saw mate trees for the first time. I had read a lot about these in the *Motorcycle Diaries*. We came across this big vine as thick as a human arm. I climbed up to about fifteen feet before realizing that I was expected to descend unassisted.

To no-one's surprise, the spoiled kids were about to cry when they were surrounded by clouds of flies. Justin and DJ Tree were covering an ear with one hand while maintaining constant motion with the other to scare off insects. The motion resembled that of DJs when they scratch disks. Therefore, they called this technique "disk scratching." The jungle takes away thousands of lives every year and therefore we decided to test its limit by wearing shorts and T-shirts and not using any insect repellents. DJ and I even wore sandals. The jungle was evidently angered by our indifference so it sent an army of mosquitoes and flies to teach us how to respect nature. We then climbed onto a three-stories-high platform and slid on a rope for a distance of eight hundred metres. It wasn't scary at all. There was really nothing much to see but trees, but it was fun.

Next, we climbed down a waterfall. This was much more of a challenge because it actually required some skills and strength. I went first and did a back flip by accident. In the end, everyone made it down safely. DJ Tree let out a roar of excitement when two girls aged between ten and fifteen got wet in their white T-shirts. It was debatable that he was in fact concerned for these girls, but I reminded him that child molestation is a serious crime in most developed countries.

We stopped by a handicraft store that sold tribal weapons. They had bows, arrows and pipes that shot needles. I thought about buying one, but I tried the pipe and it didn't work too well. I was not buying weapons that weren't strong enough to make people cry. I only shoot to kill.

We got back to Hostel-Inn at around noon for lunch. Then, we spent the whole afternoon sitting under the sun, playing billiards, soccer and ping-pong. Although it did get quite hot in the afternoon in Iguazu, the pool was cold beyond belief. No-one of a right mind would ever swim in it voluntarily. It had a unique shape: an oval with a circular "island" in the middle. Based on its temperature and geometry, I came up with an evil idea that we should put others' belongings, for example Justin's PSP, Lulu's Dior, etc., on the "island", so that they would have to experience the Ice Age in order to retrieve them. I was glad that I came up with the idea before somebody else did, but I never put it into practice because I would probably have to end up retrieving the items myself. At 4pm, we watched England draw with Sweden. Two-two. Both teams were through to the next round.

Lulu, Justin and I played a 3-on-3 soccer game in which we were annihilated. I was pissed but I blamed it on the dark. After we had all showered, we went to a restaurant they recommended, named "La Ruela", supposedly the best restaurant in town. It had the atmosphere of a restaurant but the food was ungodly; the hostel staff probably recommended it as an act of revenge. DJ's steak was well done, even though we specified "a punto", which I think is medium rare in Spanish, but I could be wrong. Justin's starter came after his entrée. Brian and I ordered two different chicken dishes both drowned in enough white wine to give Brian an adorable blush. Not me though because I have high tolerance.

Afterwards, we went to a hotel casino. We played roulette as always.

Back in the hostel, Brian and I played each other in chess and the game lasted more than an hour. It ended in a draw. We went out by the pool to watch stars. It was cloudier than the night before but it was still beautiful. I showed DJ Tree the Southern Cross and the Scorpion.

"Tarzan is handsome, Tarzan is strong."
Gerald, Forest of Iguazu, Argentina. Photo by Justin.

Gerald Yeung, Wannabe Backpackers

21st June
Pouring
Iguazu

Forces of Nature
I want to stay close as close to the edge as I can without going over. Out on the edge you see all kinds of things you can't see from the centre.—Kurt Vonnegut Jr.

As advised by the staff, we woke up at 7am to find out about our boat trip, only to realize that we needed to wait another hour for confirmation. Very often, I was the first person to get up and naturally I would be expected to deal with things. Usually I wouldn't mind but my inner evil often told me otherwise. Not being able to resist his persuasion, I would wake the others up even though their presence was not required. Lulu asked me why I did that. I had no clue either. I blamed inner evil for exploiting my jealousy.

"Why do you have to wake me up?"
"Because I am an ass-hole."

At 10.30am, they finally confirmed our trip. It has never rained that hard since Noah built his ark. The heavy rain, together with the blinding lightning and the gusting wind, persuaded us that God had abandoned humanity, again. But we could not leave Iguazu without seeing the Falls. It was another risk we brave hearts were willing to take. Whatever, I was prepared to get sick. We grabbed a quick lunch at the cafeteria, took extra pills of vitamin C and got into a taxi. The driver asked us something in Spanish, which I believed meant, "You guys still seeing the Falls in this weather?" "Shut up," was my brief response in English. Initially, I meant it as a joke. But the fact that I said it in a language he understood implied that I subconsciously wanted him to stop talking. No shit, we were seeing the Falls, what else would we be doing there? But if his question was intended to be humorous, he probably would have appreciated my humour. Anyhow, it bought us half an hour of golden silence.

We got out of the taxi and bought raincoats to wear. I don't usually even use an umbrella, but today, rain-gear was absolutely essential. We went to the pier in a roofless jeep. The entrance and the signs closely resembled those in *Jurassic Park* (actually the weather too if you remember *Jurassic Park 1*). The road to the shore cut through a thick forest, and this, together with the background storm, made me feel as if a T-Rex would jump in front of us any second.

The speedboat ride was the highlight of Argentina, storming upstream towards La Garganta del Diablo, creating wave after wave. It was going at such a high speed that the rain felt like hail on our faces. The boat went underneath several tiny Falls, which left me completely soaked and cold. We each took a dumb picture that cost US$5. I knew it was a rip-off but I still followed the others. There was a guy on the boat making a video of us all. I could not believe that we actually considered paying thirty dollars for that video, and sadly we did. It was completely ridiculous but somehow they all wanted it so I had to chip in involuntarily. They didn't question the purchase until they saw the video later that night.

For your information, Iguazu Falls is situated between Argentina and Brazil. And supposedly, the view from the Brazilian side is much nicer. We probably would have gone there if we had had visas. We went ashore and walked around for an hour, going to different lookouts and taking a lot of pictures. Everyone was exhausted and longing for a hot shower.

We all got onto a bus except for Lulu who wanted to see more. He took the train and went to La Garganta del Diablo by himself. He told us later that we had missed out on the most beautiful scenery he had ever seen.

Meanwhile, we went downtown to drop off our laundry, which was sorely needed as the last time we wore clean clothes seemed like a distant dream. We made it back just in time for Argentina vs. Holland. As usual, what appeared to be the most exhilarating fixture on paper turned out to be the least exciting game of all. A goal-less draw.

There was a BBQ at the hostel that night. The meat was disgusting. The steak was too tough even for canines and the sausages were very salty. The cocktail they provided, which I believed was rum with lemonade, tasted more or less like straight hard alcohol. The feast was a failure.

Brian and I had a rematch in chess before we went out to Cuba Libre, a local disco. Brian stayed in because it was past his bedtime. At first glance, the disco was small and the majority of people were much older than we were. After downing a litre of beer each, we started dancing. The good thing about clubbing in a foreign country is that you have nothing to lose or to worry about. I pretty much performed every single move I recalled from the movies (especially *Napoleon Dynamite*) as well as from all the material I dug out from the "Dance Dance Revolution" section of my archive.

When we took a beer break, people from all over threw us unfriendly stares, signalling us to leave. I didn't blame them because at one point we were having a contest to see who could come up with the gayest posture. Lulu won with a horny face, lips shaped like a heart while squeezing both his nipples. Utterly disturbing. I was surprised that no-one launched bottles across the room to hit him. At first, we were just playing among ourselves. Eventually, people began to join us and girls came to play with us because we were crazy. Bad girls. In general, people were very friendly and passionate. I enjoyed this party much more than the one at that giant disco in Buenos Aires. Although Cuba Libre was nothing more than a small rundown bar, it had the most welcoming atmosphere. People would join to do group dances and would never hesitate to invite any strangers and teach them. I got to dance with many different girls (even a guy too, involuntarily). I enjoyed partying in a small town like this, where you don't have to put up with acts of pretentiousness from materialistic individuals. It showed the simplicity of their community. In comparison, I find the social scene at home a little hostile. Hong Kong people love to gossip. In such a small city, it is hard to find a party without familiar faces. Very often, these people will tell the world about your "crimes". Choosing between reputation and going wild for a good time, most people choose the former; the price of doing outrageous things is too costly. For those who don't care about reputation, they hit on girls shamelessly for obvious reasons and it is almost painful to watch. Besides, hot-tempered Hong Kong teenagers' end half of their parties in fights. Don't these people come out for a good time?

    This group of amazingly hot British girls came next to us and started dancing and we sort of played hard-to-get. By the end of the night, we wanted to have our photographs taken with them. Justin pulled one of them aside.

    "My friend (pointing at me) thinks that you look like Keira Knightley," said Justin shamelessly.

She looked as if Brad Pitt just showed her the ring.

    "Oh, really? But I have brown hair!" (Yeah, no shit.)

    Although she tried to be skeptical, her giant smile betrayed her. I guess Justin deserved success after having to cover his conscience to tell such a big lie in the most natural way. Atypical of his norm, DJ Tree seemed nervous about asking this gorgeous blonde girl and so I did it for him. After accomplishing our tasks, we left immediately to spare embarrassment. I told everyone that we shouldn't be scared because we would never ever see any of them again after tomorrow. But I jinxed it.

The Iguazu Falls. Iguazu, Argentina.
Photo by Louis.

Gerald Yeung, Wannabe Backpackers

*The excursion. Iguazu, Argentina
(L to R) Louis, Gerald, Brian, Justin, Pierre.*

*No idea who she is! Iguazu, Argentina.
(L to R, back) Louis, Pierre, Justin, Gerald.*

Gerald Yeung, Wannabe Backpackers

22nd June
Sunny
Iguazu to Buenos Aires to Lima

Here Without You

When shall we three meet again? In thunder, lightning or in rain?—William Shakespeare, *Macbeth*, Act I, Scene (i)

I woke up at 9am still hammered. Things went a little out of control last night. After a shower, I woke everyone up to pack. When I went up for breakfast, I saw those British girls from last night. Apparently they were leaving too. To avoid awkward situations, I didn't talk to any of them. I was sure they felt the same. What made me a little bitter was that each of them had only a backpack of luggage, which, according to the dictionary definition, qualified them as "backpackers". I hate to admit that these girls were tougher than we were. Check out took two seconds and I became a Hostel International member for fun.

Our level of alert has evidently gone down since the beginning of the journey. At first, we never left doors and windows unlocked, put everything important in safes, stored money in multiple locations. Now, we have learned to become relaxed travellers (I avoided calling ourselves "backpackers" because our trip was considered luxurious for many). It was a good thing if anything, until we started checking out late every time, making last minute arrangements and such. Very soon, we suffered the consequences.

We were hanging out outside the hostel, enjoying the sunshine and personally celebrating sleeping in a wet bed no more. We saw a bus drove out of the driveway before us but we didn't let anything interrupt our fiesta. Five minutes later, when the ecstasy expired, someone said out of the blue, "Was that bus our ride to the airport?"

Yes, it was indeed. Fortunately, the hostel felt obliged to

provide taxis to take us to the airport. We saw the 1st half of Italy's game against Czech Republic (which Italy won two to nil and advanced with Ghana). We arrived at the Buenos Aires domestic airport by 2.30. We then went to the International airport, where Justin and Lulu left the group to spend their last afternoon in Argentina enjoying every bit of the capital's glamour. Well, it wouldn't be their last afternoon here after all. The three of us sat down at a café for lunch and watched a very entertaining Brazil vs. Japan game. Brazil played at ease throughout even though Japan scored first. Ronaldo's double and goals from Gilberto and Juninho sent Brazil to the last sixteen. Afterwards, we did some last minute souvenir shopping and decided to check in early. There was some confusion regarding the airline and it turned out that we had to go to another terminal. The other two were still nowhere to be seen. At the check-in counter, we were informed that our flight had been scheduled to leave an hour earlier, which suggested that Justin and Lulu might have to extend their vacation in Buenos Aires.

Words were inadequate to describe the complexity of our emotions, but our immediate reaction said it all: laughter, cheers and high fives. We were drowned in exhilaration but, at the same time, disgusted at ourselves for celebrating others' misfortunes. Maybe we needed time away from each other? Maybe humans naturally prefer times of chaos? I don't know. But before I could find a moral justification, the celebration was well underway. We took a picture underneath "Puerto 11", the gate at which Justin and Lulu would stare futilely for the next few hours or days, searching for traces of our departure. If I really had to analyze their undoing, the Pandora's box was the duo of Avenida Florida and Mr. Christian Dior. Materialism had once again triumphed over our feeble minds, this time at the expense of Justin and Lulu, who was called Mainland Man for a reason.

To record this historic moment, I took out my video camera for the first time in a week. I zoomed into the TV monitor

Gerald Yeung, Wannabe Backpackers

"AR —Lima —2364 —Final Call"

To gain credibility for the documentary, I needed footage from an expert in the field giving professional insight into the situation. In this case what I needed was the lady at the gate stating the cold hard fact that, "The next flight to Lima is tomorrow". But she refused to get involved in the imminent conflict among us five.

Meanwhile, Lulu and Justin were probably bragging about their great purchases and mocking us for missing out. They had no idea what was ahead of them. This reminded me of the lesson of the Machu Picchu drink. Right now they were still at the flowery tunnel catching butterflies, about to be captured by their destiny.

Up till this point, we could still live with our consciences because we had not directly exacerbated the crisis; but the *status quo* abruptly changed when we urged the lady to close the gate so that our friends would miss the flight. The few minutes, waiting for the plane to leave, felt like an eternity. At the first jerk of the aircraft, I was actually happy for Justin and Lulu to be able to acquire a better understanding of the city they loved so much. I began to hum Auld Lang Syne to commemorate our lost companions while looking at the two empty seats and already picturing Lulu cursing wrathfully and Justin yelling at the airline staff, the only flaw in the picture being that they wouldn't understand a single word of English.

In the meantime, we were sitting on a plane heading to Lima, leaving behind two comrades as POWs in Argentina. There was absolutely nothing we could do to help them besides acting sorry when we were eventually reunited, which we imagined would be days from now. Although I was lucky enough not to be involved, I felt just as lost as they were. Today, I came face to face with my ugly side, celebrating the mishap of two of my best friends.

But after all, I knew that they were more than capable of dealing with the situation themselves, if not, American Express would do the rest. Besides, hardships make experiences more memorable. Easy for me to say, I know, but hey, I wasn't the one who couldn't say "no" to shopping.

Well, I would surely miss their angry looks when they learned about the flight change. That would possibly be one of the funniest things ever and I was disappointed to be missing out. But I would wait patiently at a beach on Margarita Island, sipping champagne and hoping for the best. God-speed, brothers.

Gate Number Eleven. Buenos Aires, Argentina.
(L to R) Gerald, Pierre, Brian.

Gerald Yeung, Wannabe Backpackers

23rd June
Sunny
Lima to Caracas to Porlamar

Las Quinceañeras
Summer afternoon—summer afternoon: to me those have always been the two most beautiful words in the English language.
    —Henry James

We arrived at Lima airport for the third time and had six long hours to kill, which went by fast with the help of pizza and Big2. To say that the flight to Caracas was terrible was an understatement. Aeropostal, by far the worst airline I know of, printed their boarding passes by hand. And when that happens, you can see bad news on the doorstep. We were kicked out of the assigned seats and had to switch multiple times before the stewardess was happy. We had not slept properly for a long time, but every time when images of Lulu and Justin crossed our minds, we knew that we had no right to complain. At Caracas, this guy who claimed to work for Aeropostal escorted us to catch our flight to Porlamar. His other services included booking a four-star hotel and finding a good deal on cambio. We were probably "washing black money" for them. There was a minor problem regarding our flight booking but we handled it like professionals. In the end, the guy asked for twenty dollars from us. We yelled at him for abusing our trust and sent him away for five bucks.

    At the gate, we met these girls from Columbia who were staring at us as soon as we arrived. Brian spent a fortune on candy while DJ and I picked our preys. After talking to them, we found out that they were in a program called Las Quinceañeras, in which fifteen-year-old girls from all over Columbia go on vacation to Isla de Margarita. Wow, I wish our country did that for us when we were fifteen. Some of them were really cute and looked more mature than teenagers. Despite the high concentration of hot girls on the plane, we slept through the entire flight.

We arrived, got our luggage, bought the return tickets and headed to our hotel by taxi. When we arrived at Hotel Tropical Refuge, which was like a mile from the beach (instead of the hundred metres that they claimed), packed with old, fat people, we knew we had come to the wrong place. Usually, I would just stick with prior arrangements to avoid further trouble, but this time, there was absolutely no way in hell I was spending my dream Caribbean vacation with fifty-year-olds in this prison. After half an hour of bitching at the agent, we finally set things straight and headed immediately to Playa El Agua.

Our resort, Puerta Del Sol, consisted of several complexes of hotel rooms, two giant pools, several open bars (at the pool and at the beach), two restaurants and a tropical environment. What made it even better was that those Las Quinceañeras girls were staying at the same resort. We were about to take a dominating lead in our photo competition.

We wasted no time. I jumped in the pool right away and utilized the open bar to its full potential. Polar, the local beer, was light and refreshing, perfect for the tropical climate. Afterwards, Brian and I went to the beach to see the sunset. While we were holding hands, enjoying Caribbean twilight and discussing our prosperous future, the girls came over and invited us to play with them in the water. Please tell me that it was not just some sick dream. Things could not have gone any more smoothly. Brian backed out while I had a great time. Here I am, hand in hands with adorable company, flowing wherever the waves took us under the pictorial sunset. You know how people say that when you are in love everything is lovely and perfect? I think that was it for me. It was a scene I would never forget. Hours ago, Margarita Island was still a myth to me, but this place and I fell into instant camaraderie. By the way, Brian and I didn't actually hold hands. I had to fabricate a little romance that this journal is lacking.

The barbecue dinner was okay. I didn't eat much. We were

Gerald Yeung, Wannabe Backpackers

drinking by the pool when some adults invited us to see a dance show, which was a waste of time. We returned to the pool and continued drinking. At this hour, our minds did nothing except brainstorm ideas to seduce the maidens. We thought we were stuck with yet another shameless approach of DJ's until the girls took the initiative and asked if they could sit down. I started to wonder if they were angels because they could obviously read our minds. Please do. It was like talking to my friend's little sisters, but I found it entertaining. They asked a lot of questions about our lives and we learned a lot about theirs too. Only one of them—Sara—spoke English and so she had to translate for us the whole time. They said that even though English class was a requirement at school, their English was still, "so, so". I found that respectable because it showed how much they took pride in their language by not compromising the "universal" trend. We stayed away from sarcasm because they probably wouldn't get our humour. I refrained from saying anything rude and obscene, even though DJ Tree insisted that I ask them if they were virgins. From their perspective, I was twenty-five, Pierre twenty and Brian seventeen. They had a problem pronouncing my first name and so they called me Christopher.

In Wonderland. Margarita Island, Venezuela.
(L to R) Brian, DJ, a girl, Mafe, Gerald.

Gerald Yeung, Wannabe Backpackers

24th June
Sunny
Margarita Island

Definition of Adventure
The point of travelling is in the journey itself, not in the arrival: and similarly in the occult what counts is the search, the asking of questions, not the answers found in the cracks of a bone or the lines in your palm. In the end, it is always we ourselves who give the answer.—Tiziano Terzani

At 10am, we met up with the girls at the beach. Mafe (DJ's angel) could easily win Ms Universe in her bikini but Sara (Brian's goddess) still looked like a five-year-old.

Playa El Agua was a typical nice beach: fine sand, warm water. Looking at the Atlantic Ocean from the shore, I saw the wonders of the world for the first time. Miles beyond our vision lies a sea of opportunities and unknowns. Reincarnation contradicts my Christian belief, but if it exists, I should have been a pirate or at least a sailor in my previous life. Just imagine living among the ranks of Marco Polo, Captain Hook and Captain Jack Sparrow. "Yo ho yo ho! A pirate's life for me." Technology has undermined the modern perception of the world. We have built aircraft that can take us anywhere on Earth within twenty-four hours. They surely provide efficient and safe travelling, but at the same time, they conceal the glamour of our planet. As we fly across the oceans, miles underneath us live thousands of beautiful islands that seem to have no significance as far as our journey is concerned. The modern definition of travelling is to get from point A to point B with the quickest means, visit everything worth seeing and fly back a.s.a.p. to get back to work Monday morning. Although we are "travelling" efficiently, we miss half the fun, which is the voyage itself. A flight could hardly count as a voyage because it lacks the element of surprise. What fun is life without surprises? Although I was never a seaman, I love the idea of sea voyages because there is no fixed arrival date—one can make as many stops as desired. Imagine the hundreds of creatures one can find on any unknown island, new people one can meet and paradises one can discover in an open ocean. How can you see enough of these marvels when you have to compete with time? On top of that, the dangers of storms, typhoons and ferocious wild beasts constantly keep one within the reach of death. This is the way life is meant to be. Tiziano Terzani said that a sea voyage is more adventurous than land travel because the ocean wipes out all traces of exploration, which retains the mystery of the ocean. If the idea of exploration doesn't interest you, think about crazy stories you would have to impress girls, instead of the plain old "this one time I got so drunk that I peed on myself and passed out face down in a toilet bowl." "When was the last time you did something for the first time?"

"Christopher!!!" Columbian girls woke me up from my "pirate-want-to-be" dream and brought me back to the world where swimming in a storm is considered suicide. They wanted to fight waves ten yards offshore. I guessed I would have to settle for these modern adventures for now.

Sara left early so I became the translator. I had a problem explaining the meaning of "joke" so I decided not to tell any. We took some pictures, buried DJ in sand, and headed back for lunch. My hair band broke by accident so that's the end of metrosexuality for me.

We had hoped that this tropical paradise would provide an escape from reality but it appeared that paparazzi have infiltrated every corner of the world. Random girls would blatantly take pictures of us in public. One time, I was walking through a hallway when a girl took a picture of me with her flash, her face close to mine. It was so blatant that I had to be blind not to notice. I wonder which magazine I would make the cover of next week. But again, I didn't mind because it boosted my ego. It's only human nature to be attracted to beautiful things.

We then watched Argentina beat Mexico in OT from Maxi Rodriguez's screamer, which had my vote to be the goal of the tournament. We got henna tattoos at the beach. I liked the one on my left forearm a lot. I can already see myself getting a real one very soon. My parents would be proud to hear that.

The lowest point of a perfect day had to be the arrival of Justin and Lulu, whose place in our hearts had long been replaced by Columbian mistresses. They recounted their adventure and told us how Caracas was a dead town. We really should thank Lulu for insisting that we should come to this island. We invited Mafe and Andrea to dinner. When Sara's name was mentioned at the table, Brian blushed and confessed his love. Ooorrr, how cute.

After dinner, we drank as fast as possible and headed to Kamy Beach. You can guess the location of the club from its name. Ironically, we weren't allowed to set foot on the beach. Security was strict—I had to borrow Justin's ID to get by. We paid ten dollars to get in, but they gave us water bottles for free beer, which we utilized to their full potential by feeding beers to the children all night.

I liked all the Columbian girls. In particular, Laora was my love. Appearance can be deceiving, but in her case, you could get a fairly accurate read of her character. Wearing braces didn't seem to bother her in the least, as I never saw her without a giant grin. She was probably the best dancer I know of; I never found dancing that fun. But what ultimately mattered were the kind heart and the sense of humour. Enough of the portrait of a lady. Back to Kamy Beach. After about ten rounds of beer, I finally got a little tipsy and we started going a little crazy (robot dance and such). But unfortunately these girls did not respond to craziness as much as we would have hoped so we looked like idiots. But I didn't care. A group of Columbian boys arrived and they were a bunch of douchebags. They tried to act cool by chugging whiskey straight from the bottle. I had a sip and it tasted like expired gasoline. Why were they doing that to themselves? By midnight, a group of models arrived with their cameramen. People kept taking pictures of them but I didn't find them that hot.

    The girls had to go home at midnight. Who doesn't want to be Cinderella? At that point the disco was beginning to fill up with people closer to our age. Choosing between staying at the club and going back with the girls, we chose the latter because they promised a party back home. When we returned to Playa El Agua, we realized that it was a dirty lie. Meanwhile, Justin started a fight with Columbian boys in the bathroom. It was pretty stupid. He picks a fight when he is bored; his aggression almost never ends in bloodshed. Had it actually happened, I would have jumped right in since I had nothing better to do. The only thing that would hold me back was the Physics teacher escorting these kids. He was very nice and I didn't want to put him in a difficult situation. After all was settled, I decided to go for a swim even though it was prohibited. Sara was telling me not to because I would get sick. OKAY. Like I would listen to a fifteen-year-old. My mum couldn't have stopped me. "Hago lo que quiero." ("I do what I want"), I told her as I took off my clothes and dove in. Justin hopped in too. Brian was going to join before Sara held him back. You know, I love Brian, but sometimes he needs to be a man. I guess his hands were tied when he was trying to make a good impression on her. Oh, well.

    The security people kicked us out of the pool very soon. The girls had to go to bed and I didn't try to keep them. Now that I knew them better, I treated them as friends and cared about their feelings. Lulu and Justin disappeared.

    So it was the three of us again sitting by the pool under the starry sky.

Gerald Yeung, Wannabe Backpackers

25th June
Sunny
Margarita Island

Butt Pirate of the Caribbean

If you are young and you drink a great deal it will spoil your health, slow your mind, make you fat—in other words, turn you into an adult. —PJ O'Rourke

I was going to wake up at 7am to swim the alcohol out of my system, but I couldn't resist the temptation of food. After breakfast, I sat by the pool to write my diary. A few girls came by and talked. They asked me to write their names for them in Chinese. They thought our language was beautiful.

At 11am, we watched one of the most boring games—England beating Ecuador with David Beckham's free kick. I also wrote a couple of postcards to Gerald and Virginia. When I went to the clubhouse to send them, the girl who worked there thought my handwriting was good. I told her that it was only as pretty as she was, hoping that the compliment would ensure safe arrivals of my postcards, which unfortunately only did the exact opposite. She definitely kept them together with my four thousand Bolivares postage. I can only console myself that the cards meant more to her than to me. The word on the street was that my autograph could feed a family of four for a week on that island. Then we had lunch, but the heat spoiled my appetite. Afterwards, we swam, played volleyball, and headed to the beach. Since the girls had their own activity that day, lying down and drinking seemed to be the best option. I love the Caribbean—the palm trees, beach, ocean, people, everything. But whether I could live there all my life, I have reservations. Although my current rock star life may suggest otherwise, I have always wanted to retire to oblivion one day and lead a simple life. But what good is life without excitement? Maybe that mind-set will change as I age.

Gerald Yeung, Wannabe Backpackers

But as much as I hate the city and all its implications, a part of me is inseparable from the urban environment I grew up in. Therefore, the Caribbean could serve only as a tropical refuge for me. Sometimes, I wonder what it would have been like to grow up in a different world, say on an unknown island. Maybe I would have lived a happy, modest life, and be proud of my origin, religion and ancestry.

Brian jumped in the sea in his new white bathing suit, only to realize that the fabric turned transparent in water.

"Can you see through these shorts?" Brian asked.

"Dude, don't ask me. I am not looking," I turned my head away before finishing the sentence.

He went back to the shop and purchased a brown pair, figuring that brown should be safe. That was my assumption too until I saw manhood between his legs. Gross. He went back for the third time. This was very typical of Brian to be making the same mistake over and over again. Anyhow, they should start making bikinis like that.

Pierre, Brian and Lulu went jet ski-ing. I am not a big fan of water sports therefore Justin and I sat on the beach enjoying the scenery and tropical cocktails. An oyster guy came by and sold us fresh oysters (he opened them right in front of us). When the beach began to quiet down, we went back to the pool and played Bums, a game that involves juggling and the loser gets shot in the ass by all participants. It was a lot of fun but it got vicious at times. People around enjoyed watching us too.

The girls came back from the safari late afternoon. Mafe seemed to have met a new male companion. I felt bad for DJ Tree who had to watch them make out in the pool. Later on, the girls invited us to play in their private pool. Of course Justin sat on the side acting cool. For a moment, we went back to a third-grade birthday party. We splashed each other between giggles and the fact that we were overwhelmingly outnumbered by females suggested that we could have found heaven just now. Had we stayed longer, we would be invited to their pillow fights and pajamas parties, which I wouldn't mind because it was nice to be a child again.

We had dinner with the girls and went to a show at el teatro, where we were forced to participate in "Whisky, rum, tequila." It was a dancing game: whisky was stop; rum was switch partner and tequila the girl crawls between the boy's legs, and bananamama was homosexuality (guys with guys). Brian won the competition and got us a bottle of rum. We felt like we had done enough dancing so we sat by the pool again.

At some point, a big guy in a yellow Inter jersey came up to me.

"Hola, Spanish?"

"Un poco."

Then he asked if I liked dancing. "Yes." He asked me how many friends I had in my party. "Four." Then he stopped beating around the bush and asked if I wanted to go to a disco that night, or something along that line. He pointed at two women, one was probably his mother and the other was either his sister or friend or girlfriend. Whatever she was, she was really, really hot. Well, she was not one of those drop dead gorgeous girls who would win Ms Universe, but she had the Eva Green look that suggested that there was much more underneath the surface. She winked at me and gave me an I-want-you smirk. "I am in for sure." Later that night he came by, again acting unnecessarily intimate—he was rubbing my back while he talked. Now I had to re-evaluate our previous conversation. On second thoughts, my suspicion wasn't at all far-fetched. He got excited when I told him I had four friends (*translation*: "a party with a lot of boys"). I also forgot to take into account that my Spanish was far from good. He probably intended to ask, "Do you like dancing . . . with me?" That would be a clear indication of butt-piracy.

By the end of the night, the girls wanted us to write them something in Chinese. It was fun to exchange messages in different languages. Brian fell deeply into the abyss of overflowing love when he read Sara's message. It said something like "You like me. I love you. Remember me." I only remembered it because he recited it like five times that night.

DJ wrote for Mafe, "You are an angel," which could not be further away from the truth, given her exciting social agenda. I ran out of creativity very soon so I started writing outrageous messages like "I love you more than I love myself," "You are my hero," etc. A girl freaked out when she saw, "I want to have your baby," on her paper. I had to explain that it was an example of American slang and didn't quite mean what it says, literally.

Finally, let's talk about these huge dumb Columbian boys. Born to make everybody's life harder, they would not stop singing to us, asking idiotic questions while we tried to say goodbye to our friends. Their teachers were responsible for bringing a tribe of uncivilized monkeys out of the country to drink twenty-four/seven. They needed to be destroyed. Unfortunately, the girls were really scared of fights and I thought we should respect them. Otherwise, none of them would be going back to Columbia in one piece. This kid in braces kept asking me the dumbest questions. And then he tried to impress the girls by speaking French. Ha. We can speak French too, dipshit, much better than you too. Then he asked me what other languages I speak, I said Arabic. I made up some really throaty words and claimed that it meant, "Hi, I am Gerald. Nice to meet you."

This other idiot in a yellow polo shirt insisted on singing me a song. He also wanted his name written in Chinese, and so I wrote several curse words on his arm.

Gerald Yeung, Wannabe Backpackers

26th June
Sunny
Porlamar to Caracas to Miami

Best Seafood in Miami
You can call her an outdoor girl if she has the bloom of youth on her cheeks and the cheeks of youth in her bloomers. —Anonymous

Our day started before sunrise (thank God we didn't count on the morning call). The resort had a completely different look in the morning without its usual crowd, nonetheless as charming. I liked its tranquil environment no less than its passionate Carribbean side. We all wished to stay longer, partly because of the pleasant environment and mostly because of the lovely company even though I was unwilling to admit it. Pierre savored the purity of first love once more, while I cherished the candid friendship. Brian was clearly in love. I don't know what was in Lulu's and Justin's minds because they were only here for a day. I would love to keep in touch with the girls, but a good memory is more than I can ask for. Saying goodbye was not easy—which version of "goodbye" carries enough meaning for a friend you will never see again? I simply told them that I would miss them a lot; I have been abusing that phrase all my life, but this time I truly meant it. I whole-heartedly wish them the best. So, my recollection of Margarita Island will consist of a lot of palm trees on the beach, the blue ocean, the warm summer sun in the clear sky, a lot of Spanish, and those jolly faces. We have already started making plans to return for every year's Las Quinceañeras. It will be an annual pilgrimage to meet Columbian Señoritas. We may age with time, but the girls on the island will remain at the same blooming age. Neverland is not so hard to find after all.

    As soon as we arrived at the Marriott in Miami, we watched the overtime and shootout between Ukraine and Switzerland. We then went down to the lobby and asked the concierge what to do etc. Justin mentioned seafood restaurants, figuring that seafood here should be good.

"Forget about the restaurant, this is where you get all your seafood (pointing at a nightclub)," suggested the Hispanic receptionist.

Our expressions registered nothing but shock. No-one was really expecting that.

We went to the Red Lobster for dinner and came back to swim in the freezing pool. I went into the hot tub for a bit until the heat upset me. We took turns to do our laundry, which hadn't been done for a week. DJ had both of his cell-phones stolen from his luggage. It was very unfortunate but—to look on the bright side—that was the only incident of theft throughout the trip.

"Ciao, Isla Margarita!" Margarita Island, Venezuela.
(L to R) Gerald, Justin.

Gerald Yeung, Wannabe Backpackers

27th June
Hot as fxxx
Miami

Don't Bother to Read this

Boredom is the feeling that everything is a waste of time; serenity, that nothing is.—Thomas Szasz.

It was a rather boring day. In fact, every day we spent in Miami was doomed to be uneventful for the underaged.

I sat on the balcony trying to read the paper until I was overwhelmed by the heat. We then had to walk for fifteen minutes under the baking sun before we found a deli for brunch. We watched Brazil beat Ghana three-nil. Afterwards we went to a supermarket where Justin bought female hair products. Sometimes I wonder how we could be friends.

The rest of the day was uneventful. We sat around until the next World Cup match on TV. I wished we had changed our tickets and stayed on Margarita Island for longer. We already missed them. I hope they were feeling the same. The Spain vs. France game was sort of entertaining, but I would have loved to see Spain advance.

For dinner we went to a Chinese buffet. That was the highlight of the day.

We went back to watch The Hills Have Eyes in the hotel room. It was not scary at all and the ending was terrible. At first we thought about seeing Hostel instead but we decided against it due to the possibility of staying in one in Africa. Several days from now, we would be very proud of that decision.

Gerald Yeung, Wannabe Backpackers

South Beach
28th June
Cloudy
Miami to London

Business Class My Ass
Hello. My name's Forrest Gump. People call me Forrest Gump.
　—Forrest Gump

In my physical diary, the page dedicated for 28th June is blank, which summed up an exotic day. But for the sake of consistency, I will give a brief summary. I will make it as painless as possible to read.

　　We went shopping to kill time. The only interesting thing we saw was the Bubba Gump restaurant, started by Forrest Gump.

　　In summary, our vacation in Miami was painful. At first we had hoped to go to The Bahamas but that didn't happen. I am pretty sure I won't go to Florida again in the near future even for the spring break. Getting around was very expensive because we had to take taxis all the time; car rental was not a privilege for twenty-year-olds. I was glad we were finally leaving.

　　At the airport, I didn't hesitate to ask the lady if she would be kind enough to upgrade me to business class. She admired my outspokenness and told me that I would be rewarded. Everybody else was jealous. One has to fight for one's felicity. I deserved what I got.

　　When we finally got on the plane, we realized that we were all sitting in economy plus. I think what that lady meant was that she had upgraded all of us. They all started teasing me, which I well deserved because I was a bitch to them earlier.

Gerald Yeung, Wannabe Backpackers

Millennium Wheel, London, UK.
(L to R) Pierre, Lulu, Justin, Gerald, Brian.

More like Backpackers.
(L to R) Justin, Lulu, Pierre, Gerald, Brian.
The Houses of Parliament, London, UK.

Gerald Yeung, Wannabe Backpackers

29th June
Sunny
London to Nairobi

A Day in London
Airplane travel is nature's way of making you look like your passport photo.—Al Gore

Today, Justin turned twenty. As a friend, I am ashamed of the travel arrangements. On such an important milestone of his life, he had to spend half of it taking us around a city he has seen a thousand times, and spending the other half in a smelly British Airways cabin. I tried my best to prevent it from happening, but in the end it didn't work out. I am forever in debt.

Our visit to London was brief. As soon as we arrived, we went to the apartment where Justin lived during the academic year and showered there. This turned out to be one of our rare good decisions. Justin's friend, Jenny, who was subletting the place for the summer, had left it in such a mess that it was impossible to make it any worse. Even so, I could see her screaming at the top of her lungs when she saw the dirty bathroom and all the towels we had used. We stormed "her" place like a hurricane and left.

We then toured around the London School of Economics (LSE) campus, which only took us about two minutes. We had lunch at a Chinese restaurant and shopped at a big department store for soccer jerseys. Although I am usually a big fan, I couldn't find anything I wanted. Just when we were about to leave, Lulu insisted on our staying longer to check out the polo shirts. We didn't name him Mainland Man for no reason.

We had an objective in London—buying tents for the safari trip. Although our stomachs were urging us to get dinner instead, we decided not overlook its importance because it might be crucial to our survival in the wild. We would be reimbursed anyway. But the thought of having to bring our own tents haunted me. I mean, should we bring our Land Rovers too? There were so many unknowns ahead of us but I was ready for anything. Isn't a safari supposed to be an adventure?

We took the Heathrow Express to the airport, picked up our bags, and went to another terminal. Our flight left at 8.25, but we didn't get to the check-in counter till 7.30. Now we just had to wait in line behind forty people. After being bitched at by British Airways staff, we cut the entire queue and went straight to the counter. Just as we thought we had cleared the final obstacle, they gave us more: the flight was overbooked and Justin was picked to stay behind for the next flight to Nairobi the next morning at 10am. His birthday had already been miserable and I was not going to let it get any worse, so I volunteered to switch with him. Justin thought that no-one should be left alone and so the two of us stayed together. The others proceeded to the gate while we waited at the Customer Service Desk, hoping to get onto the waitlist for the same flight. Meanwhile, I was doing Sudoku to relax and kill time. I wasn't particularly worried because I was mentally prepared for the worst. Maybe I was supposed to be more nervous but I had a feeling that things would turn out fine in the end. At last, we both were awarded seats in the lottery and got on the flight. Before we went in, I didn't forget to give a sympathetic look to those at customer service who had to wait till the next morning to see Africa. I was such an asshole. I suggested that we should hide and pretend that we didn't get on, so as to give them a pleasant surprise, but Justin wasn't in the mood for it.

The flight wasn't too bad. Nine and a half hours. I watched *Rumor Has It*, part of *Brokeback Mountain*, and played like a hundred games of Sudoku.

Gerald Yeung, Wannabe Backpackers

*Giraffe. Kenya.
Photo by Pierre.*

Gerald Yeung, Wannabe Backpackers

30th June
Sunny
Nairobi to Samburu

We Didn't Sign Up for This
Live life to the fullest.—Ernest Hemingway

A van picked us up at the airport and drove us to the hotel to drop off some of our luggage, followed by grocery shopping to prepare for a week of wildlife. We bought about five cases of beer and four bottles of champagne; it should be a fun week. Our first destination was Samburu Game Reserve. The exotic experience began with a horrendous car ride. A four hundred kilometre journey took six to seven hours because of the poor road conditions. The ride was so bumpy that I fell out of the seat every ten seconds. The cabin accumulated an unbearable amount of heat so we had to keep the windows wide open. The tradeoff for ventilation was breathing in dirt from the road. Somehow we managed to put up with all sorts of physical torture and slept like dead men. Any mortal soul would have done so after not seeing a bed for about forty-eight hours. In some ways, I enjoyed sleeping in a cabin naturally air-conditioned by a cool breeze under the roasting sun. We woke up with sharp headaches from hours of head banging against the car.

    By sunset, we arrived at the campsite, which was a fancy name for an open area with a stove and a bench. What they called the dining room was a table under a plastic shelter. We wasted no time and set up the tents in the dark, which turned out to be much easier than I had expected. We had three tents and since no-one else wanted to sleep alone, I got to sleep by myself. This was my version of the story. Theirs was that no-one felt comfortable sleeping alone with a homo. But if that was their real concern, I failed to see how sleeping with Lulu would be any safer. Anyway, I was glad to have my first camping experience in a Kenyan safari.

Gerald Yeung, Wannabe Backpackers

There was a building fifty yards away from our campsite where people poop and shower—they called it the "bathroom". Personally I found "torture chamber" a more fitting name. It contained three stalls and no lights. One of them was a shower stall with only one switch, which had to be cold water. The other two were toilets. That night, I made a big mistake by going in with a lamp and studied the interior of the toilet bowl, which was a shallow wooden box with a circular opening on top. Whatever goes in stays in. The content of the box transformed the urge to poop into an urge to vomit. Brian asked what I saw. I only lowered my head and stated that the sight would haunt me for the rest of my life. He seemed unnerved by my response and decided against further investigation. We came to an agreement that when the time comes (and it will), we would do it cavemen style in the wild. We would crouch down, with our butts facing each other and our eyes looking out attentively for monkeys and other predators. During the process, a strict honour code would be respected, i.e. no turning around and checking each other out. With Brian you cannot overlook the importance of establishing these rules.

A week ago, we were living extravagantly in The Marriott Plaza Hotel, Buenos Aires. Now we looked around and found no lights and had nothing to keep us entertained except for a box of warm champagne and beer, and eight men. Thank god we bought a ball in London. What did we get ourselves into? But believe it or not, we were still having a great time. Our chef Humphrey was a magician who could turn limited ingredients into delicious dishes. I guess we were not that spoiled after all. The night sky was absolutely beautiful; it was just me and thousands of stars in the entire universe; my gaze brought me to infinity. I could easily spend several lifetimes admiring the galaxy.

A leopard lazing in a tree. Samburu, Kenya. Photo by Justin.

Mama & baby elephant. Samburu, Kenya. Photo by Brian.

Gerald Yeung, Wannabe Backpackers

1st July
Sunny
Samburu

"Does Anyone Want To Pee?"
Death by starvation is slow.—Mary Austin

"Does anyone want to pee?" Justin began our day at 3am by yelling to see if anyone wanted to go to the bathroom. Apparently he had been up for two hours waiting for someone else to wake up so they could pee together. Apparently he had been up for two hours until his bladder could hold no more. They had told us not to wander around at night because hyenas, cheetahs, leopards and other ominous species visit campsites frequently. I tried to go back to bed but their giggles, talk and the occasional roars of wild beasts made it very difficult. There was a big party going on.

"There is an elephant behind your tent," Brian woke me up again. This time it was 6am.

"OK, Brian," I replied, trying to go back to sleep.

"No, really," affirmed DJ Tree.

The atypical seriousness in DJ's voice startled me. I walked out and saw two elephants eating from a tree about ten yards away. Holy shit! They told us not to leave food in the tent because elephants' noses are very sensitive to sweets. Watch out Brian.

After using the bathroom, we departed immediately for our first game drive. We saw a leopard, thousands of elephants, impalas, gazelles, wildebeests, warthogs, giraffes and Grevy's zebras. It sounded like we saw many different animals but we were just seeing the same ones repeatedly. Due to the lack of exciting scenes, we had to sleep through the majority of the boring drive. This is the problem with cheap safari tours because they can only take you to the less popular reserves with a lower animal population density. We went back for breakfast at 9am and then out again for another game drive, every second of which I spent sleeping. But I didn't miss much. Although the drives were rarely exciting, at least they provided a tolerable sleeping environment. It was preferable to the alternative of getting baked at the camp. Besides, it gave us plenty of time to talk, make jokes, etc.

Humphrey cooked us some good lunch: yams, and two vegetable dishes. We each had a piece of chicken no bigger than my thumb. For our generation, meat is far from a luxury. My father used to tell me stories about fighting his brothers over a piece of pork back in his childhood. I had always found those tales hard to believe and given my parents credit for inventing them for educational purposes. What I had been treating as fairy tales for all those years came true today. However, we didn't blame the chef because it was impossible to store meat for an extended period of time without electricity. But what I had never expected was that even carbohydrate can become a treat. If you don't eat yams, good luck with eating your own flesh to survive. Lacking the strength even to clench a fist, I threw a wicked stare at chubby Justin and Lulu. Cannibalism has never been more appealing.

It was boiling hot in the afternoon and going two full days without showering was about as dirty as I could tolerate. I put on my Speedo so that I could shower with the door open for sunlight. People from other camps were staring at me in disgust but that didn't bother me. At least I cared to shower. The cold water felt great in the heat, but probably not so good at night when the temperature drops below five degrees.

Time elapsed torturously slow for the rest of the afternoon. The tents technically worked like greenhouses in that weather, but somehow DJ Tree managed to fall asleep in them. His training in the sauna room finally came in handy. The rest of us played cards under the shade and I had to start drinking warm beer. The commercials claimed that real men drink Guinness, but I believe that drinking warm Guinness shows even more character—only complete morons would do so willingly. We played Big2 for two hours before leaving for our much anticipated game drive at which we didn't see anything new except for tall Somali Ostriches. Their erotic physique reminded me of high school cheerleaders. Their feathers covered the smallest part of their lower bodies, leaving the entirety of their thighs exposed. God gave them long and beautiful legs that human girls beg dearly for every night in their prayers. Their feminine perfection suggested that there should be no males in this species. Paul, our driver, tried very hard to look for lions but met no success. He even drove up a mountain over a path of sheer stones. It was a miracle the van did not tip over. We got to the top unscratched but I wish I could say the same for the vehicle. We took pictures at the look-out spot and gathered pebbles to attack the monkeys that persistently ambushed our tents for food.

That night, we watched Portugal beat England in penalties. Seeing Justin's defeated expressions was voted one of the best moments of the World Cup. We saw Brazil play France right after. Brazil came into the World Cup with a dream squad and everyone expected them to achieve nothing but glory. Their performance, however, could hardly live up to their reputation.

Even more like backpackers. Samburu, Kenya.
(L to R) Pierre, Justin, Brian, Gerald, Lulu. Photo by Paul.

Lake Nakuru. Nakuru, Kenya. Photo by Justin.

Great Rift Valley. Kenya. Photo by Gerald.

Gerald Yeung, Wannabe Backpackers

2nd July
Cloudy
Samburu to Lake Nakuru

Totally Didn't Sign Up For This Either
Unless you try to do something beyond what you have already mastered, you will never grow. —Ralph Waldo Emerson

We woke up at 7am to pack for departure. While Justin and I were walking towards the bathroom, the first and only thing he said to me was that he needed to shit really badly. Hang on cowboy, we were going somewhere new today and there would be hope. After breakfast, we departed for Lake Nakuru. The scenery along the way was gorgeous; seeing lots of big, flat fields inspired a soothing sense of freedom. Eventually we reached the top of a mountain and got a clear view of the Great Rift Valley, which extendes five thousand kilometres from Syria to Mozambique. Here we saw a prospering rural civilization very different from the one we are accustomed to in the city.

We picnicked there and had the worst meal ever: some sort of sandwich (tomato and cheese?), a hot dog that tasted awful, and a piece of chicken even a starving dog wouldn't lay an eye on. Was it part of the whole African experience? When we were done eating, we carried on with the journey and eventually crossed the equator, which was kind of cool.

As soon as we arrived, we ran to the bathroom and thank God it was a decent one. Nothing feels better than letting out the baggage we had been carrying for days. And by "baggage", you know what I mean. While Paul was dealing with the admission passes, we played several rounds of Bums. Meanwhile, monkeys attempted to steal from our car. We chased them away and I officially became their predator.

After settling problems with our student IDs, we managed to get into the park. We saw some Common Zebras, which were smaller and had wider stripes than Grevy's Zebras. At the lake, there were a million flamingos and seagulls. Hoping to get a closer look at the birds, we got out of the car but were repelled by the odor of rotten carcasses, which grew progressively worse as we neared the water.

We finally saw white rhinos. Paul claimed that they were "white" because they were first discovered by a white man, and that they weighed exactly 2.7 tons, while black rhinos weighed one and a half tons. There are two subspecies of White Rhinoceros (also known as Square-lipped Rhinoceros or Ceratotherium simum, whatever that means). The Southern White Rhinos, which I believed were the ones we saw, are the most abundant subspecies of rhino in the world. A population of about eleven thousand live in South Africa alone.[6] Northern White Rhino that are found in East and Central Africa, on the other hand, are critically endangered with only thirteen of them left in the entire world. Each of them carried an indispensable responsibility to extend their bloodline. Men have tried their best to help them but unfortunately they refuse to reproduce in captivity. While most people find that disheartening, I have a different opinion. What is the point of lingering in the world when you rely on others to reproduce? Besides, what good is survival, when there are only thirteen of your kind left on the planet?

Impala are one of my favorite animals in Kenya. They define style and substance. The impala's graceful bound can reach a speed of ninety kilometers an hour. Because of that, all predators (except for cheetahs) can only watch them bounce cheerfully in the wild and can do nothing to harm them. A young impala is distinguished by a black stripe on both flanks, which will completely fade away by adulthood. I prefer to recognize them by the big black "M" on their ass. My other favorite was Dikdik. It is a tiny antelope, the size of a puppy, with legs no thicker than chopsticks. I thought these animals were really cute.

After taking a million photos from the top of the hill, we

headed towards the town. On the way, I had a bottle of warm Tusker Malt Lager while Justin had a warm Smirnoff Ice. It wasn't too enjoyable for either of us. We should have thought twice before we bought them.

The moment of truth. At this point, everybody was filthy, tired, and most importantly about to shit his pants anytime after holding in for like five days. Our hopes were up when we stopped at this fancy hotel. Humphrey went in to inquire the price and came out to tell us that there was no vacancy, like I actually believed him. It was definitely just too expensive but whatever. Then we went to another one that looked noticeably worse, and I was well pleased that Humphrey came out to look for a better one. Our third attempt was the Hotel Royal Spring. After a quick glance at the building, I immediately bowed my head in prayer, "Please don't do this to me". But before God had time to answer my prayer, Humphrey started unloading our bags.

As soon as I stepped into the entrance, I saw bad news written all over the empty hallway. I was glad we didn't see Hostel in Miami. Justin and I walked up to our room, took a deep breath and opened the door. "Bang!" Our bags slammed the floor. "Oh Shit!"

The tiny bathroom contained a showerhead and a toilet bowl with no seat. The sink was located next to Justin's bed and so when I brushed my teeth, I would certainly splash water all over his face. The lack of power outlets in the room was utterly unacceptable, as all our electronic devices (iPods, cameras, PSP) sorely needed replenishment. Therefore, we each took a single instead (which had outlets). Justin, the master of bad decision making, did it again. He decided to take a shower before dinner and paid the price fifteen seconds into the process. The water stopped for some reason, leaving him with hair full of shampoo. He screamed for help while we laughed hysterically. But behind the laughter lay the worry that we would meet the same fate. I definitely didn't sign up for this.

The rest of us went to dinner. We got wind of Humphrey preparing a feast for us, which could be accurate if you consider a plate of fries and two sausages a feast for a full-grown man.

"What other dishes will we be enjoying this evening?" I inquired politely.

"That will be all," replied the waitress.

"Bring me the menu, please."

To make up for the deficiency of protein, we ordered fried chicken, chicken stew and chicken soup that turned out to be the same thing, and some cold sodas. I understood that they were working on a budget but we were way beyond the age that could be bribed by a plate of fries. They might as well not feed us. Meanwhile, Justin finally made his appearance and taught us how to shower with distilled water.

DISCLAIMER
The following paragraph contains obscene content.
Readers view at their own risk.

After dinner, the female at the reception desk told me that the water was ready for a shower. Knowing that her words should not be trusted entirely, I decided to allow extra time for the water to heat up. In the meantime, I needed to enjoy the luxury of a toilet, which I might not see again until the end of the trip. I won't go into the details but it felt good. Unfortunately, I made an amateurish mistake by courtesy flushing for myself halfway through. When I was all done, I realized that the flush took an hour to "reload." And since there was no toilet seat or cover, I had to watch and breathe in the odor of poo during my shower. Besides, throughout the entire bathroom experience, I had to leave the door open to get a view of the outside because if I looked anywhere in the bathroom for more than five seconds, I would throw up. At that moment, I wished that my brain came with a switch that I could use in times of emergency, such as this, when I needed to cut off all links to the imagination to prevent those foul images from burning permanent marks into my memory.

Of many memorable experiences throughout our journey, that shower was one that I would remember for the remainder of my life. The issue of freezing water aside, the water pressure was comparable to urination. Learning from Justin's lesson, I saved up a bucket of water for an emergency. I showered faster and faster, hoping to finish before the water ran out. Eventually, it came down in droplets, just as expected. Although I had been working with the efficiency of a robot, I didn't make it. My hope died in the process of using the soap and conditioner. With no other option, I turned to my last resort, the bucket of dirty water. I didn't want to look at it, as I knew for sure that it was anything but clean. It had never taken that much courage to lift a bucket. I poured it all over myself hoping to wash away anything that did not belong to my body. Then I sprinted out of the bathroom, and, banging the door shut, buried my tearful face in the pillow and swore I would never step inside it again. That was one of the worst things that has ever happened in my life. By the way, I hate to disappoint you, but the crying part didn't actually happen; I figured tears would make the scene little more dramatic.

Later that night, I finally had reception on my cell-phone and my parents called a couple of times. They were desperate to learn how I was after my disappearance from the face of the Earth for the past few days. I assured them that I was in good spirits even though personal hygiene and other mundane health issues remained concerns. For your information, calling Hong Kong costs forty dollars a minute.

We enjoyed the luxury of electricity and watched a movie. Afterwards, I couldn't fall asleep until like 3am, thanks to the blinding light in the hallway. Besides, something serious was happening in the animal world—cats and dogs barking and moaning, chasing after and fighting each other all night. I thought I heard deaths. Dogfights in Kenya were very vicious.

Zebra socialising. Nakuru, Kenya. Photo by Justin.

Buffalo. Nakuru, Kenya. Photo by Pierre.

Gerald Yeung, Wannabe Backpackers

3rd July
Sunny
Lake Nakuru to Narok, Masai Mara

Reefer
I tried marijuana once. I did not inhale.—Bill Clinton

At 7am sharp, I woke up, packed and left that shithole immediately and never looked back. I had the continental breakfast, which provided one edible item—Spanish omelette. Afterwards we embarked on a six-hour drive to Masai Mara. Lulu forgot to return his room key so he just threw it out of the window, which was kind of mean. Before I left, I asked the girl at the reception how the hotel was assessed in the five-star system. She simply looked away; I took that as a "zero." Paul asked me if I had had a good night's sleep. "Of course," I replied sarcastically. "Me too," he said in a most satisfied tone. Besides the difference in skin colour, we were a universe apart.

We stopped at Narok for lunch. The entrance to the restaurant was less than enticing. We had to pass through a butcher's shop, where a huge dead cow hung at the window. Then we walked through a dungeon, past a sinister courtyard with all four sides surrounded by three-storeyed fences. It reminded me of prisons in movies where lifers lean over the balcony to watch whatever goes on in the courtyard: slaughter, sacrifice . . .. Just as I was about to tell Humphrey to go elsewhere for food, he led us upstairs to a room that looked reasonably clean. The food was not bad and we did not leave a single piece of meat on our plates.

Paul had to take the car to the garage, so we had a chance to shop around and met a girl who custom-made necklaces for each of us. I think her name was Janet. When Paul returned with the car fixed, she ran over to say goodbye and wished us a good safari trip. Something I really like about Kenya was that everyone speaks English exceptionally well and is extremely friendly with tourists. We continued the uncomfortable drive and passed through a few villages. How do local children spend their summers? These villagers obviously don't have cars and they are at least two hundred kilometres away from everything. Maybe the concept of summer holiday doesn't exist when school is a luxury. They probably look forward to school more than we look forward to holidays. I guess in their free time, they herd cattle, run around the mountains, and breathe in fresh air all year long. I would probably find it relaxing for about a week before going insane. But I don't feel bad for them because they all seemed very happy. Besides, I have always been a zealous advocate of the no-school campaign. Throughout my life I have been convincing my parents that school is propaganda.

    We arrived at the campsite in Masai Mara at 4pm and were relieved that we didn't have to pitch our own tents. The tents they provided here were big enough to fit in two beds. Each tent was built under a hay roof to block off sunlight and rain. The male bathrooms were stalls with a hole on a ground while the female ones had actual toilet seats. Pretty certainly we would be using the female ones. Laugh all you want, but masculinity is a non issue at this point. The security guards at the site were locals dressed in African tribal robes. Their outfits and bald heads reminded me of Shaolin monks. Therefore I will be referring to them as "the Shaolin Temple eighteen bronze men".

    As for the game drive, there wasn't much to see other than the same species we found in Samburu. After half an hour of driving around aimlessly, we saw twenty vans stopped before a ditch. Under a tree on the other side of the ditch rested a few lions. I had brought my binoculars halfway around the world but left them in the suitcase when they were most needed. Since the lions were too far away for my naked eyes, I began checking out hot girls in other vans instead. They just happened to be just as rare as lions in Kenya.

    We went back for a few rounds of Bums before dinner. It

was spaghetti night.

After dinner, we played a lot of Big2, rotated every hundred. At some point, I smelt a distinct odor of marijuana. I turned around and found Japanese people behind us blazing (the technical term for smoking weed). One of the monks was definitely stoned out of his mind. We wanted to see stars (I saw a meteor again) until a monk crept behind us out of nowhere and scared the shit out of me. Figuring that we should keep a distance of at least twenty yards from him, we decided to call it a day and went to bed.

I wanted to change into pajamas. Unfortunately it was pitch dark in the tent and I didn't have a torch. They had reminded us on many occasions to bring bug repellents, torches and other necessities for the safari but I still chose not to acknowledge their well-meant advice. Oh well. I just took off my clothes and went to bed.

Graceful lioness. Masai Mara, Kenya.
Photo by Louis.

Gerald Yeung, Wannabe Backpackers

4th July
Sunny
Masai Mara

To Berlin!
Anyone who thinks that they are too small to make a difference has never tried to fall asleep with a mosquito in the room.
 —Christie Todd Whitman

When did we come to Alaska? I had trouble figuring out where I was when I found myself curled up into a ball in the morning. It was below-zero in the tent. The cold caught me off guard. I really should have put some clothes on last night. It took tremendous courage to get out of bed. I, however, had no right to complain compared to what Lulu had been through. He had been at the mercy of a mosquito trapped in his tent all night. Life is probably much harder for insects nowadays, thanks to all the various chemical products we have created. In all fairness, it would have been asking too much of the mosquito not to sink its sucker into Lulu's snow-white flesh at all, but was it really necessary to bite him on his pimples? The brutal combination of itch and pain constituted the insects' ultimate revenge on mankind. By the way, we had been taking pills that act to kill mosquito eggs, so as to prevent catching malaria, and this is the reason why we had been exploring the safari fearlessly in short sleeves and without bug repellents. We weren't completely stupid, you see.

    This morning, we had much better luck as we ran into three cheetahs. I will give a brief description of cheetahs and leopards. Leopards are great tree climbers and have a very stern visage and intricate fur pattern. Cheetahs are known for their pace (one hundred and ten kilometers an hour). They have a very streamlined body, long legs and flexible spine. Their fur is tan with scarce black spots.

    Then we found a beautiful wheat field that reminded me

of a scene in *The Gladiator*. There seemed to be no animals around and so we suggested getting out of the vehicle to take photographs. But Paul, our driver, immediately vetoed the idea. He had a point because we could hardly see ten yards ahead in the long and thick vegetation. Five minutes later, his prophecy came true. We found three lions (big females) under the shade of some trees and I swear I couldn't see any of them until we came within several yards. All the big names in the jungle came out to celebrate Lulu's twentieth birthday.

The lions looked much bigger when viewed in proximity. And even the female inspired an air of superiority unrivaled by other animals. Their stare penetrates right through you. No wonder the lion is considered the king of all animals.

It didn't take long before we witnessed two hyenas stealing from a group of birds. We had to thank Paul for not letting us out. People from other vans could be seeing lions and hyenas hunting five dumb boys.

As our daily routine, we went back for some Bums and Big2. We had dinner and left early for the big game. But an incident of homosexuality took place when we were about to leave. I asked Pierre to take my wallet out of my back pocket and as he did so, I acted as if I enjoyed it. We were obviously messing around, but one of the bronze men seemed turned on and ostentatiously grabbed my ass. The jovial atmosphere turned into complete awkwardness.

"What are you doing?" I threw him a firm gaze.
He stopped laughing.
"Are you serious?" I said with a straight face.
"No, just joking."
"Good, because I really am gay."
When it comes down to acting gay, I never lose.

We went to a lodge nearby to watch the World Cup semi-final game. We thought the game was at six but it turned out that kickoff wasn't until ten. Justin put WWE on TV and turned up the volume. At one point, a kid no more than six years of age came in with his mum. They were early for the game too. With no better options, they had to kill time by watching TV, which was currently showing people smashing each other with chairs, ladders, and the crowd yelling "shut the fxxx up." I felt bad for both the kid and his mum. The boy was probably asking for explanations for the animal-like behaviour on the screen and his mother, who seemed fairly uptight, was clearly not accustomed to such bloodshed. It was a little irresponsible of Justin to coerce them into such an uncomfortable situation.

Finally, Italy versus Germany. Even though the bar was crowded with Germany fans, we made no attempt to hide our support for Italy. I would have expected both sides to play cautiously but it turned out to be a highly entertaining game. A lot of chances were created, and just when the match was about to go to penalties, Grosso gave Italy the winner followed by Del Piero's finesse. To Berlin!

This is what happens when you lose in Bums. Masai Mara, Kenya. Photo by Pierre.

Attentive cheetah. Masai Mara, Kenya. Photo by Gerald.

The Great Migration. Masai Mara, Kenya. Photo by Brian.

Gerald Yeung, Wannabe Backpackers

5th July
Sunny
Masai Mara to Tanzania to Masai Mara

The Proof of Manhood
Show me the man you honour, and I will know what kind of man you are, for it shows me what your ideal of manhood is and what kind of man you long to be.—Thomas Carlyle.

We woke up at 7am for breakfast and this time we were much more prepared for the morning chill.

We weren't expecting to see anything new today because we had pretty much seen it all. Very soon, we found a group of fourteen lions eating every bit of a zebra. It wasn't as cruel as I would have thought.

We also saw hippos and crocodiles at a river but we could only see a portion of their heads from a distance.

When we finally met a grown-up male lion, something else drew our undivided attention—hot girls in other safari vans. I was taking pictures of them, checking them out with binoculars, all performed blatantly. Oh, I finally took my binoculars out from my luggage. I guess it is never too late.

Then we went to the border of Tanzania and jumped back and forth between the two countries, making fools of ourselves. Whatever. I liked how the border was defined by a simple marker in lieu of a barbed-wire fence or guards armed with rifles. It reinforced the idea of an open country that invites anyone to walk across the frontier in search of the continent. This probably had to do with the fact that animals seldom travel with passports. Lulu should really consider settling down here.

We witnessed the annual great migration from Tanzania to Kenya. Every year, thousands of zebras and wildebeests migrate between Masai Mara and Serengeti to look for green pastures. Many predators followed them to wait for an opportunity to catch weaker prey.[7] And even birds tag along to act as scavengers. It is one of the biggest parties in East Africa.

After lunch, DJ Tree and I went for a hike up to Masai Mara Mountain. Our guide, the monk who was found abusing drugs a few days ago, tried to sell us his lion tooth necklace. The tooth had the length of my hand. He told us that he, together with ten others, killed a young male lion with spears back in his youth and he was now willing to trade his special souvenir for ten US dollars. The authenticity of his heroics aside, even if he did slaughter the beast, I explained to him that the necklace meant more to him than it would to me. For me, it would be nothing more than a souvenir I bought from Kenya for ten bucks. Had he sold this token of manhood, the story behind would be lost forever. Another page would be torn from the book of human knowledge, even though the story will live forever in his memory, whether it was true or not.

"I will get my own when I kill my first lion." He got my message and never brought it up again.

The hunting images that flashed through my mind reminded me of Hemingway's, "True At First Light". Much as I admire Hemingway as a writer, I despised the killing of wild animals. Darwinism governs our society with two of the most fundamental principles: natural selection and evolution, which boils down to a simple phrase—survival of the fittest. Although we humans lack the physique to become predators and the legs to run away from them, our creator granted us unrivalled wisdom, which not only guaranteed a spot at very top of the food chain, but more importantly, allowed us to progress with evolution and history. For several thousand years, human civilization has progressed beyond the point where our existence could be threatened by other living beings, even though the quality of life is still dependent on other animals (meat, clothes, and other things). Now that predators seem to be a distant reality, we take pleasure in slaughtering them. Instead of running away from lions, we chase them, trying to conquer either subconscious fear or an ambiguous idea we called "pride". It is wrong from a moral standpoint but I guess it could marginally qualify as a process of natural selection. But if that is the case, it should be settled in a more natural manner. Unfortunately, we exploited our wisdom to create unfair advantages, forcing our opponents into combats that they have no chance of winning. Guns, arrows, traps.... Are these parts of the divine plan too? What gives us the right to combat these worthy foes with anything but bare hands, just like it has always been? People who hunt for sheer entertainment fail to realize that superficial values are concurrently triumphing over their moral judgment. Is that part of natural selection too? I don't consider sniping at a lion from fifty yards away an act of manhood. A man who lives in the presence of ferocious predators is a true champion. I am sounding like a hardcore, animal rights fighter, but I admit that I cannot survive without meat. Sometimes the contradictions in my logic amuses even me.

Back to the hike. Although the monk hadn't made a good impression on me earlier, I had to admit that he was quite knowledgeable. A lanky fellow strolling with a spear, possessing an infinitely distant vision, he introduced DJ and me to an aspect of nature which we had never seen before and made warm introductions of his "friends in nature", clearly demonstrating their specialties. For example, there was a tree with leaves that had the texture of sandpaper. There was a green plant whose leaves would turn red if friction was applied. And there was another plant that people stick under their arms as deodorants. His acquaintance with nature reminded me of Pocahontas, my favorite Disney character. It takes more than pure knowledge to develop this relationship. Perhaps this is a side of nature we city people will never understand. He told us that the name Masai Mara came from the word O Mara, Masai giraffe in Swahili. I don't know how much of that is true but it seems very poetic.

We didn't leave Africa without learning several Swahili

phrases. "Jambo", "Welcome". And of course, "Hakuna Matata", "No Worries". He truly demonstrated the essence of that phrase.

*A man who slew a lion and a boy who believed it.
Masai Mara, Kenya. Photo by Pierre.*

Club House of the Masai Mara campsite, Kenya. Photo by Louis.

Two of my best friends: DJ and Soccer.
Masai Mara, Kenya. Photo by Brian.

Gerald Yeung, Wannabe Backpackers

6th July
Sunny
Masai Mara to Nairobi

In the World of Ostriches
What do we leave behind when we cross each frontier? Each moment seems split in two; melancholy for what was left behind and the excitement of entering a new land.
—Ernesto "Ché" Guevara

We woke up at 6am for the last game drive. I hopped into the van straight from bed. Seeing lions wasn't as exciting anymore. And our new driver refused to get too close to the animals because he held himself to a high moral standard. I had no problem with that and I admired his integrity, but he complained about us falling asleep, which had become our routine at this point. Well, if we had to spot our own animals, should I drive the car too while Lulu feeds him grapes in the backseat? He did know quite a bit about wild life, I would give him that.

He showed us a tree with big sags hanging down the branches. It was called the Sausage Tree. Apparently locals add sugar and salt to these sausages to make beer, which sufficiently explained the distinct taste of Tusker beer. As painful as one could imagine, we consumed most of the alcohol at room temperature while leaving Tusker beer completely intact to demonstrate that beers cannot be brewed from sags hanging off a tree. We gave them all away to people who appreciated them, i.e. the locals.

Ostrich mating was more entertaining than many plays I have sat through in my life. When a female wants to mate, she will spread her wings as a signal. Of course we made like five thousand references and jokes about that, most of them involving THE Chinese curse word. This male ostrich wasn't putting out at all. He kept running away until the female finally gave up, to preserve her ever-so-little pride. Their gestures and expressions were so vivid that I thought I was watching a satirical drama. The human world should emulate this aspect of wildlife. I, along with all men, would strive to build the utopia where girls would hit on guys shamelessly in broad daylight with no help from substances like alcohol. Sadly enough, that is not very far from reality nowadays. The change will take away the fun but it will surely make life a whole lot easier for most people. DJ Tree promised that this would be his wish for his next five birthdays.

We then went back for breakfast and woke Brian up from his sweet dreams. After playing Bums for the last time and taking pictures for reminiscence, we said goodbye to wildlife.

The ride back to Nairobi wasn't as painful as I had expected. The road was really bumpy and dusty at first, but it flattened out towards the end. Nonetheless, we ate dirt the entire ride. Choosing between being baked alive or eating dirt, we chose the latter so we left all the windows wide open. Our shirts turned brown and our hair could stand up straight and be styled in any way we liked.

We stopped for lunch at a hotel. It was a buffet with only four dishes but the food was unexpectedly good. Then we went to the gift shop. I bought a copper bracelet for four hundred shillings, eleven hundred less than the original price. Later on, when I found out that it was worth no more than a hundred and fifty, I felt like an outwitted tourist. I thought about buying a Kenyan flag but he was asking for two thousand five hundred. I must have looked very gullible for him to make such a bold attempt to rob me. We finally arrived at Nairobi and settled down in the Kenya Comfort Hotel. George brought our luggage from the office and settled the last bill regarding the tents. We thanked each other and he hoped that not only would we spread the word to our friends, but also leave comments on the website and tell them how they can improve. Finally he stopped beating around the bush.

"So was it a dream safari?"

Gerald Yeung, Wannabe Backpackers

There was a moment of silence. While we were looking at each other waiting for somebody to respond to the sensitive question, the images of Hotel Royal Spring, toilet with no seat, sensation of cold water dripping on my head etc. all flashed through my mind.

"Everything beyond our wildest imagination," I replied without lying.

All the banks and exchange bureaus were closed at that hour but we were lucky to have George settle things for us. We bought even more souvenirs from this store manager who wanted not only customers but friends. Awwwww.... That's so cute. I thought about buying a cross pendant made of semi-precious stone according to him, but the name of this gem sounded so ridiculous that I was not ready to take such a big risk.

We thought about going to the Carnival, a grill that served all types of games. Zebras, crocodiles, impalas. . . . But we vetoed the idea due to the lack of time and cash. We dined at a decent restaurant in the neighborhood and watched a Stephen Chow movie before going to bed.

Back home in Hong Kong!

Gerald Yeung, Wannabe Backpackers

7th July
Sunny
Nairobi to London to Hong Kong

A Casa

If an ass goes travelling, he'll come home a horse.—Thomas Fuller

We woke up at 5.30am after a good night's sleep. I went down for breakfast and then we went to the airport.

At the gate, we were scanned twice in the span of two minutes and were interrogated for trivial information. DJ Tree copied down the name of the staff both as means of intimidation and grounds for complaint. Justin was about to bite people when they checked the content of his backpack, messed with his cellphones and his beloved PSP. Finally, we got on the plane without killing anyone on Kenyan soil.

Twelve hours later, we arrived at London and checked in immediately; we surely learned from our previous visit. Waiting in line with us were many high school kids desperate to go back to Hong Kong for the summer. In comparison, we looked a lot more like backpackers, with our filthy bags, long hair, wrinkled clothes and the tan. We did become backpackers in the end, sort of. It took forever to check in and afterwards we got something to eat at a restaurant. So we were finally boarding our last flight. Another twelve hours of flying may intimidate most people, but we have gotten used to it by now. We have had worse; at least this time we were sober.

Well, it is about time to go home. Hong Kong misses us.

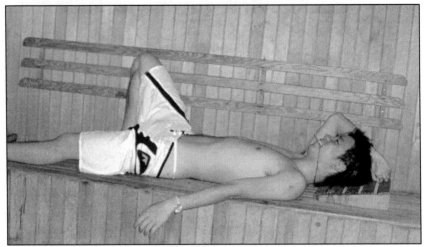

DJ Tree. Photo by Gerald. Buenos Aires, Argentina.

Pierre (DJ Tree) Speaks

After around twelve hours of flight, we arrived at Lima at around one in the morning. Without losing any opportunity to have fun, we went directly to the pub opposite the hotel after we had checked into our room. We are energizer bunnies.

I started to wonder if people had refrigerators in the restaurant in Lima. Every time we ordered, we saw them going to get the ingredients from the market. And I also wondered how much of a tip a waiter deserves if it takes him half an hour to put out knives and forks.

Why would a guy ride a bike naked? To demonstrate the correlation between penis size and friction, I guess.

I can spend a day in Machu Picchu just to purify my soul. And I really need to do that because even holy water would turn black if I bathed in it.

How cool is it to go to bars and pubs beside a graveyard (at Recoleta, Buenos Aires)? A good reason to get drunk. By the way, teenagers in Buenos Aires go clubbing after 3 a.m.

Gerald Yeung, Wannabe Backpackers

After going to Venezuela, I can tell why five Miss Worlds are from there. Together with all the fifteen-year-old girls that were staying at the same hotel with us, the island instantly became my paradise.

Getting closer to Mother Nature makes me realise how small I am in this world. Most wealthy men aren't happy. There is so much more in life that we often forget about when we live in a city.

"Is it expensive to pay ten dollars US for an hour of happiness?" "Of course, happiness is always free." Quoted from a Cantonese movie named something like "Sixth Floor's Backyard."

I prefer travelling a thousand miles than reading a thousand books because one is constantly encountering new things in a new place.

Spending nine thousand US dollars to travel for a month when I am twenty years old was not a wise decision for me. I could have saved that money for lots of other things, but if you consider the experiences I got out of this trip, it was all worthwhile.

Justin (a.k.a. "Hau Lan")
Lake Nakuru, Kenya. Photo by Louis.

Justin's Memories

When asked about our four weeks of "backpacking" or "travelling around the world" by family and friends, I don't seem to be able to tell them how amazing it was. There are just too many favourite moments to treasure and lots of hilarious stories to share. Sometimes words are inadequate to sum up this dream-come-true trip—spending a month travelling with four good primary school friends. What more can a kid ask for?

If I really had to choose my favourite moments of the trip, I would have to go with the dinner at La Rosa Nautica. On top of the sumptuous seafood meal, the reminiscent feeling that all five of us experienced was invaluable. It was like a reunion of good friends who had gone their own ways since primary school. I certainly got carried away with memories of the primary school days to an extent that I almost forgot that we were dining in a restaurant along the coastline of Lima. Not many people keep in touch with their primary school mates, let alone spend one month on vacation with them. Thus I consider myself lucky to have grown up with these brothers.

Amongst many other favourite moments, the short period that we spent on Margarita Island stood out. For others, this might be because Puerta Del Sol was the place where certain individuals rediscovered the feeling of first love or found Girls, as I strongly emphasize, that they will marry in ten years' time. For me, it was the carefree time spent on Playa El Agua. Sipping cold beer and fruity cocktails under the sun, savouring fresh oysters and appreciating the Carribean scenery at the same time, I could not find anything more relaxing. It was very near bliss. Besides, I managed to engage myself in some deep and meaningful conversations with Gerald while the others were enjoying jet skiing. Gerald and I probably know each other inside out after all these years but it was one of those rare occasions that we discussed life and tried to figure out answers to questions like,

Gerald Yeung, Wannabe Backpackers

"Where will we be in ten years' time?"

One of the biggest achievements during this trip from our point of view was opening up our dear friend Brian's little introverted world of relationship ordeals, which had always appeared to his close friends as a mystery for many years. On this trip, he has firmly established himself as the king of sentiments. This was confirmed when he exchanged excessively mushy notes with a little girl named Sarah. Although we seem to have demystified his relationship problems, there are still some mysteries that remain unsolved. What did Brian do in the hotel room (possibly on Gerald's bed) when the others went out for late night activities? What really happened when he shared a room with Gerald in Cusco?

Apart from extraordinary shopping behaviour, the possession of illegal documents and the hundreds of self-portraits of Lulu in Machu Picchu, I would treasure the days we spent in the tent the most, catching up with each other's social life, school life, and love life. Lulu never fails to say things that you would remember for life. These are the exact words: "Justin, you know we gotta inform each other exactly when we are gonna have children in the future, so our children will be the same age and can be good friends as they grow up together." I mean, you've got to be close friends to say that to somebody.

The innocent little boy called Lam Ying that used to attend all my birthday parties back in primary school is now known as the notorious DJ Tree after the tour. Lam Ying Pierre brought a lot of joy to our tour and certainly allowed us to gain a lot of insights into his fantasies. DJ Tree's bold moves will definitely be remembered and talked about for many years to come. Last but not least, I will always remember the disc-scratching technique we developed to steer clear of mosquito bites and his obsession with trapping himself inside the sauna.

Last but not the least; I believe I cannot end my summary of this wonderful trip without making a few remarks about the self-proclaimed grandmaster and warrior Gerald. But before I plunge into doing so, I feel that it really is necessary to thank him for putting so much effort into making this trip happen. Now that the thanking part is done, I can start reminding the readers about some peculiar feminine behaviour and some comical moments of the grandmaster throughout this trip.

As much as he attempted to disguise himself with his frat boy image, his true side was revealed whenever he naturally crossed his legs in many photo shots or made funny weird noises whenever he was surprised. Also I must not forget to mention his obsession with putting on moisturizers and wearing hairbands. Two weeks into the trip, I felt it was the right time to create a nickname for him. But unfortunately, it is inappropriate to share it here with our readers. Since then, I have also noticed that certain members' actions were influenced by this strange culture.

Without disclosing too much risqué detail, many of us are still scratching our heads, wondering about the night when the five of us shared a room in Miami, asking why the four of us, including Gerald, woke up with stiff backs and buttocks one morning; all except for one fellow member whose name will remain secret. This leads to my final question arising from my observations.

Why was Gerald the only one of us who had half a dozen homosexual male individuals approach him in South America? Let's not forget about the time when he was harassed by one of those Eighteen Bronze Men in Kenya.

Finally, repeating time and time again, there could not have been a happier and more fulfilling way of spending my summer than to experience this amazing and unforgettable trip with you guys. While we start looking forward to our next trip, we will have to settle for now with some hot pot and karaoke sessions in Hong Kong.

Gerald resumes his story
Epilogue

It has been two weeks since we came back from Africa with our bags covered in dust. Many of us have already pursued other plans for the rest of the summer: Justin, Lulu and Brian have begun working; DJ has been trying to get back on good terms with his girlfriend while I have been writing this diary. A month has gone by fast. The first few days in Lima felt like eternity but time has flown ever since.

"How was your trip?" We have been asked the same question repeatedly. I don't know about the others, but for me, "Good" is the best response I can come up with simply because there are so many things in my mind. I am not going to say that "our thoughts could not be described by words" because firstly, it is not true and secondly, it sounds really gay. But when I sit down and take my time to summarize everything in writing, I don't even know where to begin. Therefore, I am going to start from the most superficial aspects and progress to more meaningful ones.

Let's begin with appearance, the immediate association with superficiality. Whether it was intended or not, we have been on a successful diet but I am sure it will take Justin no time to gain his weight right back. Now we can eat as much as we want, especially for us who live in Hong Kong, the food paradise. Speaking of food, hot pot and fat beef have been haunting us ever since our visit to el Museo de Oro in Lima, especially in Kenya when we had to settle for vegetables and pasta for dinner. Last week, we finally got to do so. That was officially the end of our trip. I brought home the bottle of inexpensive champagne we never drank. Although it was cheap, I will leave it for special occasions. After all, it flew half way around the world with us.

Although we never did the exact calculations, our expense was roughly under-budget (less than ten thousand US dollars each), thanks to our habits of not paying tips, bargaining with cab drivers, overloading every cab and negotiating with hawkers over fifty cents. For those planning to go to South America, or basically any other long trips, it is a good idea to buy an Around the World Ticket, but you should purchase domestic flights separately because agents in Hong Kong are bound to rob you. Of course they will warn you that the flights will be full. Bullshit. Every time when we were black out drunk on the plane, we could always find empty rows in the centre to pass out for several hours. And there are always plenty of seats left on any flight. If not, you have a perfect excuse to extend the vacation.

To my surprise, we didn't get into major fights. There have been inevitably moments that we got frustrated at each other, but none of our deeds was intolerable. Differences come from disparity in opinion and choice of lifestyle. Although we may not appear so, we are all educated grown-ups who have spent our whole lives learning to get along with people and not to piss them off. Besides, differences reveal new dimensions of personality. We learned more about each other and I am going to share some of our darkest secrets.

Lulu loves shopping. This is no news to anyone, but who could have guessed that he would even miss a flight for it? For future reference, travelling with Lulu should be avoided it there is an alternative, or at least one should stay away from taking the same flight to avoid collateral damage when the Mainland Man is arrested for using illegal documents. By the way, his parents never found out about his visa episode.

Justin appears to be the most mature of us all, but under the red hair and the never-smiles-when-he-takes-picture face lives a ten-year-old boy diagnosed with a tendency for domestic violence. Honestly, twelve-year-olds are too old for WWE, but Justin refuses to let it go. Forget about the wrestling game he spent days on, whenever he saw a pool, a bed, a mattress, basically anything remotely resembling the surface of a wrestling ring, he would turn to one of us with the look of a poor kitty and ask, "can I please Rock Bottom you?"[8] I mean, any person of the right mind would say "no". Well, maybe not DJ because his reasoning cannot be analyzed by common logic. The only time we fed the monster was when I cheated in Bums and took a Rock Bottom as part of my punishment.

Another person who needs to be rescued from Neverland is Brian. There is nothing wrong with eating candies, but don't try to convince me that consuming a daily Toblerone for thirty consecutive days could be any good for his health. On a more serious note, things between him and this girl are complicated and it is too long a story to be told here. Exactly how long? Probably just a little shorter than his phone bill. Nonetheless, I wholeheartedly wish him the best with his young girls. "You like me. I love you. Remember me. Love, Sara."

I like making gay comments, but at times I have taken this a step too far, almost to the point where people around me feel threatened. Why do you think I got my own tent every night in Kenya? Some say that I am highly selective when it comes to girls. The word on the street is that I am turning gay because fat, manly girls with braces are hard to find. I disagree. Anyhow, I am not responding to that.

Lastly, Pierre is a strange puppy. Perhaps we can blame it on the fact that we knew him the least to begin with, but DJ Tree never failed to surprise us with his weird hobbies. In order to make this article suitable for all audiences, I have had to leave out most details. He loves Japanese girls; this is the only politically correct fact I can share. Toes, handcuffs what, DJ? He also has no shame in asking random girls for pictures, which won him the contest. After all, setting the age limit was not enough to prevent him from winning. By the way, DJ didn't wear underwear for the entire month, which we found disturbing whenever his ass crack was shown. It also made me a little uncomfortable when we did our laundry together but I won't make too much fun of him because he gave me all his disposable underwear since I forgot to bring any.

    We were grateful about coming back in one piece. We bought travel insurance, which never came in handy, except maybe when DJ lost his cell-phones in Miami (watch the rhyme). I find it hard to believe when people warn me not to travel because of the danger of an alien environment. Accidents are as likely to happen at home as anywhere else. Besides, where is the fun in a life without risks and surprises? Some will call that an irresponsible attitude, but I am all for adventure.

    The World Cup was not as exciting as I would have hoped, but I could not be happier with the result: Italy being the new world champion. At first we were worried about missing most of the action. It would be a costly sacrifice for us soccer fans. Fortunately, soccer, or football, whatever you call it, possesses an unmatchable charisma. Everywhere we went, people would abandon their engagements and stand religiously before the TV to feel the excitement of the game, even though they couldn't name a single player on the field. In Africa, people would walk miles across villages to the nearest TV just to watch twenty-two men kick a ball around for ninety minutes. We felt football anywhere at anytime. While we were waiting at any airport, there was always a TV showing the game. Even on the plane, we were often awakened by sudden "GOOOLLLLL!!!!!" announcements. This has been said like a zillion times but I feel like it is the right moment to state the obvious.   Football is THE universal language. I have never been more proud to be a football fan.

    Sometimes, we are too caught up with the rarity of success in life and we often take family and friends for granted. Our friendship is constantly under exigent challenges. In the most urgent circumstances, such as one when two of our friends were about to miss a flight, instead of doing whatever it takes to prevent the gate from closing, we almost pointed a gun to the pilot's face to coerce an immediate departure. But even after what we did to each other, we were still very good friends, just like it has always been since Primary One. If you find that hard to believe, here is the evidence: how often can you not kill a person after seeing him for thirty consecutive days?

From not having visas in Los Angeles to missing a flight to Lima, we decided not to inform our parents of our troubles. There was no point making them lose sleep over their sons five thousand miles away. I have never had children myself and so it would be unfair of me to comment, but I think that parents always exaggerate problems because they underestimate our abilities to a certain degree. I cannot speak for others, but in our case, we have five spectacular actors and experienced liars. We have talked ourselves out of trouble from teachers and peers in countless occasions. The secret to lying is to master the art of self-deception. "To deceive others, you first have to deceive yourself." In discos, we gained confidence by telling ourselves that we were the coolest kids in the world. I know lying is bad, but even the most honest person tells lies. Why is the person you see in the mirror always good-looking?

Lastly, we learned an important lesson from the Columbian girls. Perhaps we might not have understood a word they said, but it was always nice to see them. Whether it was eight in the morning or eleven at night, they were always laughing, smiling, and having a good time. They created a joyful atmosphere that inspired happiness in the people around them, and together with the blue sky and ocean, there was not a worry in the entire world. Maybe this is why people choose the Carribbean as a retreat from reality. But why can't life be like this every day? Why do we enjoy ourselves only on vacations? I believe it has to do with the people more than the environment. The climate and the scenery are surely charming, but what is a paradise without the people? The laughter sends a cordial invitation to relax mind and body. Seeing troubled individuals in the street yelling into their cell-phones, you can almost feel their concerns in the air. So if you are smiling every day, you are doing the world a huge favor.

Gerald Yeung, Wannabe Backpackers

That is the daily philanthropy I contribute to humanity.

Did we come back changed? I can't speak for the others, but public bathrooms finally became my friends. Although we were desperate to go back to civilization, we all seemed to have adapted to the simple and quiet safari life. Personally, I have since been reluctant to go out to crowded and noisy places. I simply don't want to deal with people. Maybe African monks inspired me in seeing through the superficiality of the material world. Finally, we understood the essence of the appellation—the accolade—that we have been chasing, "Backpackers". It is not about how un-luxurious the trip was and the number of nights sleeping on the street. True backpackers are explorers, who travel with an open mind. Although we were still somewhat spoiled and considerably naïve, we came as close to being backpackers as we ever could.

When will we go on vacation together again? I don't know, but I hope I won't have to wait too long. Maybe we can go to Columbia to visit Sara. Hopefully she will turn into a fine woman. By the way, Brian actually kept in touch with her. A Euro trip seems to be another popular choice but I am open for suggestions. Can we be real backpackers next time?

So that was what happened in summer 2006, the year we turned twenty.

What we had in common: our restlessness, our impassioned spirits, and a love for the open road.
—Ernesto "Che" Guevara

Gerald Yeung, Wannabe Backpackers

We hope you will see us again!
Margarita Island, Venezuela.

Mucho gusto en conocerlos, me calleron muy bien, y les coji aprecio, son muy interesantes y buenas gentes.

Very nice to meet you all, you made a good impression on me, I care for you all. You are interesting and good people.

Los quiero
(I love you)
Att: Mafe :)
Bogota, Colombia
25/06/2006

About the Author

Gerald Christopher Yeung was born in Madera, California on 29 April 1986. He grew up with his younger brother Clement in Hong Kong where they both attended St. Paul's Co-educational College.

In Form Four (Tenth Grade), Gerald transferred to Lawrenceville School in New Jersey for the last three years of high school. At Lawrenceville, he competed in the Lawrenceville Swim and Soccer Teams and he was named a New Jersey First Team All-State Swimmer in 2004. He graduated from Lawrenceville, *Cum Laude*.

He subsequently graduated from Cornell University in spring 2008 with a bachelor degree in Mechanical and Aerospace Engineering.

Gerald speaks five languages with a varying degree of fluency, Cantonese, Mandarin, English, Spanish and French. This has played a pivotal role in his travels and ultimately his becoming a writer.

He first gained exposure to writing during a summer internship at Saatchi & Saatchi, where he worked as a research assistant for *Sandy Thompson*, author of *One In A Billion*. Since then, he has been dreaming about becoming a writer himself one day. What stood between him and his first book was the lack of an interesting topic. In summer 2006, the opportunity finally came when he made a back-packing journey with four of his best friends, namely, Justin, Louis, Brian and Pierre. The idea of writing a journal about their travels came from *The Motorcycle Diaries* by Che Guevara, who toured Latin America on a motorcycle.

Gerald's journal does not inspire a desire for revolution like Che's work. It brings out the lighter side of Latin America in the tone of a spoiled teenager. It was originally intended as a gift for the families who sponsored the trip. But a year after he

Gerald Yeung, Wannabe Backpackers

finished his manuscript, he decided to submit it to publishers and he promptly received a positive reply from Proverse Hong Kong. That has since opened up a new, exciting world for him.

Gerald has recently begun working for Pall Corp at Cortland, New York. While his professional career will be his prime focus, writing will continue to play a big part of his life. One day, he would like to be a full-time author. Meanwhile, he is writing a childhood memoir. He has also finished the first draft of a book that speaks the satisfaction of finding a home and family in a Latino country during his volunteering trip to Costa Rica in 2007. Then in the summer of 2008, upon graduation, he backpacked around Italy and southern France to numerous cities and towns, including some wineries where he learned about wine, and this experience will also soon appear in writing. (As you can see, he believes in multi-tasking.) There are more ideas in the works, so one can expect to hear from him again and again in the near future.

To keep in touch with what Gerald is doing, please visit:
Gerald's website: www.geraldyeung.com
Gerald's blog: www.geraldyeung.blogspot.com
All information supplied by the Author.

The Portfolio

Oh yeah, almost forgot about the contest. Here are some of the nice girls we met!

Columbian Señoritas. Margarita Island, Venezuela.

Gerald Yeung, Wannabe Backpackers

She who sold me pyjamas. Aguas Calientes, Peru.

Happy Times. Kamy Beach, Venezuela.

Gerald Yeung, Wannabe Backpackers

DJ. Cusco, Peru.

Gerald & Ms Laora (L). Brian & Ms Sara (R).
Margarita Island, Venezuela.

Gerald Yeung, Wannabe Backpackers

DJ with a model. Kamy Beach, Venezuela.

Pretty Peruvian girls. Ollyantas train station, Peru.

Gerald Yeung, Wannabe Backpackers

Ms Mafe and DJ. Margarita Island, Venezuela.

Gerald Yeung, Wannabe Backpackers

Ms Mafe & Pierre. Kamy Beach, Venezuela.

Pierre & Ms Esperenza. Margarita Island, Venezuela.

Gerald Yeung, Wannabe Backpackers

Margarita Island. We love Venezuela!
(L to R) Brian, Pierre, a girl, Mafe, Gerald.

Justin. Lima, Peru.

Gerald Yeung, Wannabe Backpackers

Cuba Libre of Iguaza, Argentina.

Justin and pretty English girl. Cuba Libre of Iguazu, Argentina.

Gerald Yeung, Wannabe Backpackers

Gerald with Ms Scholars. Lima, Peru.

Glossary and References to Art, Games, History and Movies

<u>Auld Lang Syne</u>: a song people often sing on New Year's Eve. In many cultures, the song is used to mark a farewell and say goodbye.

<u>Bar Crawl (*slang*)</u>: an activity involving going to bar after bar until only one person is standing.

<u>Batman (*movie*)</u>: Alfred: Batman's butler who looks old but reliable and gentle.

<u>Big2:</u> a card game. Some people call it Hong Kong/Chinese poker. It is called "Big2" because two is superior to every card in the deck including the Ace. The objective of the game is to get rid of all your cards as soon as possible. It is too difficult to explain the rules of the game here. If you ask every teenager in Hong Kong, he/she will teach you, and possibly make some money from you, once you are hooked on the game.

<u>Blaze (*slang*)</u>: to smoke marijuana.

<u>Bums (*game*)</u>: A ball-controlling game involving any part of the body except for the arms. The goal of this game is to keep the ball in the air. Players are allowed to take as many touches as possible. They can also pass the ball to other players as long as it doesn't touch the ground. But when a player drops the ball, he gets a penalty in the form of one of the letters B-U-M-S- in that order B-U-M-S. The first player whose penalties complete the word BUMS has to stand in an assigned place, and then bend over with his butt facing the other participants, who each take a shot with a soccer ball at the loser. And they are entitled to kick as hard as they can.

<u>"DJ Tree"</u>: See note 3.

<u>Harry Potter Series (*movies*)</u>: "Well done, Ms Granger. Five points for Gryffindor." In the Harry Potter series, being the most precocious student at Hogwarts the wizardry school, Ms Hermione Granger often tries too hard in answering questions.

Sometimes, she could not resist yelling out the answer even when she was not asked.

<u>Hau Lan (Justin's nickname)</u>: a derogatory nickname Justin came up with. Literally, it means "back door" but it is a euphemism for "butt piracy". I shall not clarify the explanation, but please feel free to look up "urban dictionary" if you feel inclined to do so. At first it was intended for people we didn't like, but we soon started using it to address each other. Since Justin used that on me the most, I thought that it would be appropriate to retaliate by slipping the title into his contribution of the book without his consent. Justin doesn't particularly like to be called with this name.

<u>Haul ass (*slang*)</u>: to travel very fast, usually in a vehicle.

<u>Home Alone (*movie*)</u>: In this movie, Kevin McCallister stayed at a luxurious hotel without his parents and charged a long list of expenses to his parents' credit card. (Staying at the Marriott in Buenos Aires)

<u>iPod</u>: a electronic device produced by Apple Inc., capable of storing every song you ever knew, in your pocket. It plays music in several audio formats, including the best known, MP3. For a time when it was less popular, owning an iPod would give you a certain social prestige. Nowadays, it has become extremely popular among different age groups in many countries.

<u>Jurassic Park (*movie*)</u>: In *Jurassic Park 1*, the dinosaurs managed to escape the bounds of the electric fence during a storm and this led to turmoil.

<u>Leonardo Da Vinci's Last Supper</u>: one of the most famous paintings of Leonardo Da Vinci. The subject of this painting is the last meal that Jesus shared with his twelve disciples before his death.

<u>Lighthouse of Alexandria</u>: regarded as one of the Seven Wonders of the Ancient World, located on the island of Pharos in Alexandria, Egypt. With a fire and reflective mirrors at the top of the tower, the lighthouse served as a navigation landmark during

the 1st century AD.

MacDonnell Road, Hong Kong: where both our primary school and our secondary school are located.

Napoleon Dynamite (*movie*): a comical movie that talks about the life of a high school reject named Napoleon Dynamite. At the very end, Napoleon managed to impress the whole school with a choreography performance during the election campaign for his best friend Pedro.

PSP: short for Playstation Portable. A handheld video game console manufactured by Sony.

Pussy (*slang*): Pet name for a cat. In this book, it means a coward. Be careful with its use because I have heard it has a different meaning and it can be very vulgar.

Rock, paper, scissors (*game*): The simplest game in the world. On the count of three, each player shows one of the three symbols (rock, paper or scissors) with his/her right hand and the winner is decided based on the following rules: paper beats rock; rock beats scissors; scissors beat paper. The symbol for rock is represented by a clenched fist; paper by an open palm; scissors by a clenched fist with the index figure and the middle finger pointing out. This game can be played by a minimum of two and a maximum of five people.

Rock Bottom: The signature body slam of The Rock, an American wrestler.

Shaolin Bronzemen: This comes from a few Hong Kong movies, but the only one our generation knows is *God of Cookery* by Stephen Chow. In that movie, the eighteen Shaolin Bronzemen were extremely unpredictable individuals who would beat up anyone at will.

Stephen Chow is perhaps the funniest person in Hong Kong. He was first an actor, but today he is also an internationally-known producer. His movies, especially the earlier ones, will have you in tears even on a blue day. He is our hero.

Sources of information

Discovery Channel. Peru (Insight Guides).
Guevara, Ernesto Che, *The Motorcycle Diaries*, (London: Harper Perennial, 2004).
New Scientist. Welcome to Sun City, Peru, http://www.newscientist.com/channel/earth/mg19025524.000-welcome-to-sun-city-peru.html, accessed 4 August 2006.
Wikipedia. Machu Picchu, available from http://en.wikipedia.org/wiki/Machu_Picchu, accessed 3 August 2006.
Wikipedia. White Rhinoceros, available from http://en.wikipedia.org/wiki/White_rhino, accessed 5 August 2006.
Tanzania Safari and travel to East Africa. The Wildebeest Migration, available from http://safari.go2africa.com/africa-features/wildebeest-migration.asp, accessed 1 August 2006.

Notes

[1] New Scientist. *Welcome to Sun City, Peru*, http://www.newscientist.com/channel/earth/mg19025524.000-welcome-to-sun-city-peru.html, accessed 4 August, 2006.

[2] Ernesto Che Guevara, *The Motorcycle Diaries* (London: Harper Perennial, 2004), p.104.

[3] One night when we were playing Big2 in the hotel room in Lima, Pierre was in charge of playing songs from an iPod. The selection was horrible. Afterwards, Justin realized that Pierre had deleted most of the songs from the iPod by accident. After this, we sarcastically nicknamed him "DJ [Disc Jockey] Tree".—"Tree" is the last word of his Chinese name.

[4] Discovery Channel. *Peru* (Insight Guides), p.228.

[5] Wikipedia. Machu Picchu, available from http://en.wikipedia.org/wiki/Machu_Picchu, accessed 3 August, 2006.

[6] Wikipedia. *White Rhinoceros*, available from http://en.wikipedia.org/wiki/White_rhino, accessed 5 August, 2006.

[7] Tanzania Safari and travel to East Africa. *The Wildebeest Migration*, available from http://safari.go2africa.com/africa-features/wildebeest-migration.asp, accessed 1 August, 2006.

[8] "Rock Bottom" is the signature move of The Rock.

Books published by or available through Proverse Hong Kong
www.geocities.com/proversehk

*Also from The Chinese University Press of Hong Kong, The Chinese University of Hong Kong, Shatin, NT, Hong Kong, SAR, China. Email: cup@cuhk.edu.hk
#Also available or soon to be available in one or more E-book editions.

*THE COMPLETE COURT CASES OF MAGISTRATE FREDERICK STEWART AS REPORTED IN *THE CHINA MAIL*, JULY 1881 TO MARCH 1882, 2008. CD. Preface by The Hon. Mr Justice Bokhary PJ, Court of Final Appeal. Edited by Gillian Bickley. Indexed by Verner Bickley. Supported by the Council of the Lord Wilson Heritage Trust. ISBN-13: 978-988-17724-1-1.

"Together [these brief reports] do even more for the modern reader than put him in the armchair of someone who took the *China Mail* in Victorian Hong Kong—although that alone would be interesting enough. They provide him with a seat at the back of Mr Stewart's court, alive again and in session."— The Hon. Mr Justice Bokhary PJ.

CULTURAL RELATIONS IN THE GLOBAL COMMUNITY: PROBLEMS AND PROSPECTS, 1981. hbk. 255pp. Edited by Verner Bickley and Puthenparampil John Philip. ISBN-10: 81-7017-136-9; ISBN-13: 978-81-7017-136-2.

*THE DEVELOPMENT OF EDUCATION IN HONG KONG, 1841-1897: AS REVEALED BY THE EARLY EDUCATION REPORTS OF THE HONG KONG GOVERNMENT, 1848-1896, ed Gillian Bickley. Hong Kong, 2002. hbk. 633pp., inc. bibliography, index. The only collected, corrected, annotated, introduced, published edition of important source materials, with brief biographies of four of the writers *and archival photographs*. Supported by the Council of the Lord Wilson Heritage Trust. ISBN-10: 962-85570-1-7; ISBN-13: 978-962-85570-1-1.

"An essential resource for those researching colonial education policy." — Norman Miners, University of Hong Kong, in, *The Journal of Imperial and Colonial History*.

*# FOR THE RECORD AND OTHER POEMS OF HONG KONG, by Gillian Bickley, 2003. pbk. 118pp. w. author's portrait. Sixty poems written during a residence of 30 years in Hong Kong. With a talk given to the English Society of the University of Hong Kong. *With two CDs of all poems read by the author.* Supported by the Hong Kong Arts Development Council. ISBN-10: 962-85570-2-5; ISBN-13: 978-962-85570-2-8.

"A perceptive account of life and people mostly in Hong Kong, rendered with empathy, humour and surprise."—Agnes Lam.

"Thought-provoking and entertaining." — David Wilson, *Sunday Morning Post*, Hong Kong.

*# FORWARD TO BEIJING! A GUIDE TO THE SUMMER OLYMPICS, by Verner Bickley, 29 February 2008. pbk. 260pp. w. 16 b/w photographs & author's portrait. ISBN-13: 978-988-99668-3-6.

"Explains for each Olympic Sport the rules, special terms & vocabulary. Lists impressive Olympiad achievements of the past. Contains fascinating insights into the history of the Games. Showcases the Beijing Olympics, the third Asian Summer Olympiad. Provides for visitors, & residents of Beijing & Hong Kong useful information, phrases, dialogues, quizzes and conversational openers."

"Comprehensive and scholarly. The idea is noble: encourage visitors to embrace the symbolic gesture of this third Asian summer Olympiad—international goodwill, cooperation and peace." — *Hong Kong Magazine*.

"Will appeal to the adult 'armchair enthusiast' seeking to get the most out of televised events. Appeals across age and gender, designed for longevity." — Vincent Heywood, *Chinese Cross Currents*.

E-book edition (2008): ISBN-13: 978-988-99668-7-4

*# THE GOLDEN NEEDLE: THE BIOGRAPHY OF FREDERICK STEWART (1836-1889), by Gillian Bickley, David C. Lam Institute for East-West Studies, Hong Kong Baptist University, 1997. pbk. 308pp., inc. bibliography, index. The biography of the Founder of Hong Kong Government Education and first headmaster of Queen's College (then the Central School), *w. archival photographs*. ISBN-10: 962-80270-8-5; ISBN-13: 978-962-8027-08-8.

"Dr Bickley's life of Frederick Stewart is beautifully written, eminently readable, and at times moving." — Lady Saltoun.
"We need more studies of this type to understand fully the complexities of colonial rule." "[I] thoroughly enjoyed this book." — Clive Whitehead, University of Western Australia, *Int. J. of Lifelong Education*.
"Bickley tells the story with unswerving admiration and many vivid touches." — Douglas Hurd, *The Scotsman*.

*THE GOLDEN NEEDLE: THE BIOGRAPHY OF FREDERICK STEWART (1836-1889). Full audio version on 14 CDs. Read by Verner Bickley. ISRC HK-D94-00-00001-40.

Also, TEACHERS' AND STUDENTS' GUIDE TO THE BOOK AND AUDIO BOOK OF 'THE GOLDEN NEEDLE: THE BIOGRAPHY OF FREDERICK STEWART (1836-1889)': Proverse Hong Kong Study Guides. Mobipocket E-book. ISBN-10: 962-85570-9-2; ISBN-13: 978-962-85570-9-7.

JOCKEY, by Gillian Bickley (when Gillian Workman). pbk. 64pp. Written for young readers. Based on extensive research. Authentic background to the RHKJC. Suitable as a reference for adults interested in the history of the then Royal Hong Kong Jockey Club. Original illustrations. ISBN-10: 962-85570-3-3; ISBN-13: 978-962-85570-3-5.

*# A MAGISTRATE'S COURT IN 19TH CENTURY HONG KONG: COURT IN TIME: Court Cases of The Honourable Frederick Stewart, MA, LLD, Founder of Hong Kong Government Education, Head of the Permanent HK Civil Service & Nineteenth Century HK Police Magistrate. Contributing Ed., Gillian Bickley. Contributors: Garry Tallentire, Geoffrey Roper, Timothy Hamlett, Christopher Coghlan, Verner Bickley. Preface by Sir T. L. Yang. Modern Commentary & Background Essays *with* Selected Themed Transcripts, 2005. ISBN-10: 962-85570-4-1; ISBN-13: 978-962-85570-4-2. pbk. 531pp. inc. bibliography, index, notes, w. 56 b/w archival illustrations.

"The contributors have written with insight and understanding ... a most readable book." — Sir T. L. Yang. "[The] lengthy introduction ... is a masterly and impartial survey." — Bradley Winterton, *Taipei Times.*

E-book edition, 2005, revd 2008 with the new title: A Magistrate's Court in Nineteenth Century Hong Kong: Court in Time: the Court Cases Reported in *The China Mail* of The Honourable Frederick Stewart, MA, LLD, Founder of Hong Kong Government Education, Head of the Permanent Hong Kong Civil Service & Nineteenth Century Hong Kong Police Magistrate. Modern Commentary & Background Essays with Selected Themed Transcripts and Modern Photographs of Heritage Buildings of the Magistracy, Prison and Court of Final Appeal. ISBN-10: 962-85570-7-6; ISBN-13: 978-962-85570-7-3

*# MOVING HOUSE AND OTHER POEMS FROM HONG KONG, by Gillian Bickley, 2005. pbk. 130pp. With a talk given in the English Department Staff Seminar Series at Hong Kong Baptist University. *With one CD of all poems read by the author.* ISBN-10:962-85570-5-X; ISBN-13: 978-962-85570-5-9.

"The variety of human life and the individual response to life, these are Gillian Bickley's central interests." — Emeritus Professor I. F. Clarke and M. Clarke, UK.

* MOVING HOUSE AND OTHER POEMS FROM HONG KONG, TRANSLATED INTO CHINESE, WITH ADDITIONAL MATERIAL by Gillian Bickley, Edited by Tony Ming-Tak YIP. Translated by Tony Yip & others, June 2008. pbk. 140pp. w. 9 b/w photographs & editor's portrait. ISBN-13: 962-988-99668-5-0

* PAINTING THE BORROWED HOUSE: POEMS, by Kate Rogers, March 2008. pbk. w. 3 b/w photographs & author's portrait. 68pp. ISBN-13: 978-988-99668-4-3.

"Ostensibly a voyage through China, Hong Kong and Taiwan, it is really a journey through the emotions." — Bill Purves, Examiner, Hong Kong Arts Development Council.

"Here is an author in her prime; confident, sure of her craft, and willing to take risks." — Donna Langevin.

*# SIGHTINGS: A COLLECTION OF POETRY, WITH AN ESSAY, "COMMUNICATING POEMS", by Gillian Bickley, 2007. pbk. 142pp. w. author's portrait. With a talk given in the English Department Staff Seminar Series at Hong Kong Baptist University. Supported by the Hong Kong Arts Development Council. ISBN-13: 978-988-99668-1-2.

"Bickley has made use of everyday life situations and turned them into life lessons. **Sightings** inspires us to slow down and taste the sense of the city." —Ma Kwai Hung, Examiner, Hong Kong Arts Development Council.
E-book edition (2008). ISBN-13: 978-988-99668-8-1

Gerald Yeung, Wannabe Backpackers

*# SPANKING GOALS AND TOE POKES: FOOTBALL SAYINGS EXPLAINED, by T. J. Martin, June 2008. pbk. 106pp. w. 16 b/w illustrations by Jacinta Read & two author's portraits (one with Sir Stanley Matthews). ISBN-13: 978-988-99668-2-9

E-book edition (2008). ISBN-13: 978-988-99668-6-7

POEMS TO ENJOY (w. sound recording of all poems), Hong Kong Educational Publishing Co. pbk. 3 vols of graded poetry anthologies (kindergarten to adult), with Teachers' Notes. Verner Bickley, editor & anthologiser. ISBN-10: 962-290-018-6; ISBN-13: 978-962-290-018-9; ISBN-10: 962-290-019-4; ISBN-13: 978-962-290-019-6; ISBN-10: 962-290-020-8; ISBN-13: 978-962-290-020-2

SEARCHING FOR FREDERICK AND ADVENTURES ALONG THE WAY, by Verner Bickley. Hong Kong, 2001. pbk. 420pp., inc. bibliography, index. w. author's portrait. The story of the book, *The Golden Needle* (the biography of the Founder of Hong Kong Government Education). Supported by the Hong Kong Arts Development Council.

Narrative of research, with useful addresses and contact information, intermixed with stories and reflections from the author's own life experience, mainly in Asia. *With archival and modern photographs.* ISBN-10: 962-8783-20-3; ISBN-13: 978-962-8783-20-5.

"Verner Bickley writes in a mostly light-hearted vein, with a gentle humour." — Sir James Hodge, British Consul General, Hong Kong.

*THE STEWARTS OF BOURTREEBUSH. Aberdeen, UK, Centre for Scottish Studies, University of Aberdeen, 2003: pbk. 153pp. Extensive documentation of the Scottish family of the Founder of Hong Kong Government Education, Frederick Stewart presenting the perspective of each family member. As such, a reference to writing family history and biography. *With archival photographs and facsimiles of documents, Hong Kong & Scottish subjects.* ISBN-10: 0906265347; ISBN-13: 978-0-906265-34-5.

Gerald Yeung, Wannabe Backpackers

About Proverse Hong Kong

Proverse Hong Kong, co-founded by Gillian and Verner Bickley as a small independent press, is based in Hong Kong with strong regional and international connections. Proverse is a member of IPHK (Independent Publishers of Hong Kong) a group set up for mutual benefit and support in 2006.

Verner Bickley has led cultural and educational centres, departments, institutions and projects in many parts of the world. Gillian Bickley has recently concluded a career as a University teacher of English Literature spanning four continents. Proverse Hong Kong draws on their combined academic, administrative and teaching experience as well as varied long-term participation in reading, research, writing, editing, indexing, reviewing, publishing and authorship.

Proverse Hong Kong has published non-fiction, poetry, young teens and academic books. Other interests include biography, memoirs and diaries, novels and short stories, and academic works in the humanities, social sciences, cultural studies, linguistics and education. Some of our books have accompanying audio texts. We work with texts by non-native-speaker writers of English as well as by native English-speaking writers.

Proverse welcomes authors who have a story to tell, a person they want to memorialize, a neglect they want to remedy, a record they want to correct, a strong interest that they want to share, information or perceptions they want to offer, skills they want to teach, and who consciously seek to make a contribution to society in an informative, interesting and well-written way.

The name, "Proverse" combines the words, "prose" and "verse" and is pronounced accordingly.

The Proverse Prize

The Proverse Prize for an unpublished publishable book-length work of non-fiction, fiction or poetry was established in January 2008.

Its objectives are: To encourage excellence and / or excellence and usefulness in publishable written work in the English Language, which can, in varying degrees, "delight and instruct".

Summary Terms and Conditions (for indication only & subject to revision).

There is a Cash prize of HKD10,000 and **possible publication**. The entry fee is HKD200 OR GBP30. Depending on the quality of the work submitted, the prize may be shared or withheld, as recommended by the judges. (HKD7.80 = approx. US$1.00)

Writers are eligible, who are over eighteen years old on 1 January of the year in which they submit their entry or entries to The Proverse Prize. There is no nationality or residence restriction.

Each submitted work must be an unpublished publishable single-author work of non-fiction, fiction or poetry, the original work of the entrant, and submitted in the English language. Plays or school textbooks may not be submitted and are ineligible.

Translated work: If the work entered is a translation from a language other than English, both the original work and the translation should be previously unpublished.

Extent of the Manuscript: within the range of what is usual for the genre of the work submitted. It is advisable that fiction (e.g. novels, short-story collections) and non-fiction (e.g. memoirs, essay collections, biographies, autobiographies, etc.) should be in the range, 80,000 to 110,000 words. Poetry collections should be in the range, 8,000 to 30,000 words.

Writers may choose, if they wish, to obtain the services of an **Editor** in presenting their work, and should acknowledge this help and the nature and extent of this help in the Entry Form.

KEY DATES FOR FIRST AWARD OF THE PROVERSE PRIZE (*subject to confirmation)

Deadline for receipt of Entry Fees/ Entry Forms	30 May 2009
Deadline for receipt of entered manuscripts	30 June 2009
*Announcement	September 2009-October 2009
*Award Made	December 2009-April 2010

For full & up-to-date details and Entry Form please visit the *following page on the Proverse Hong Kong website:* <www.geocities.com/proversehk/proverse_prize>.
Enquiries by email to <proverse@netvigator.com>.

Alternatively (for entries from Hong Kong), you may **request a copy of the details and entry form**. **Write to:** "The Proverse Prize, Proverse Hong Kong, P.O. Box 259, Tung Chung Post Office, Tung Chung, Lantau, NT, Hong Kong, SAR, China", enclosing a stamped self-addressed envelope (A4 size).